First Published in Great Britain in 2005 by
House of Raven Book Services
King's Sutton
OX17 3RS

Typeset in Caslon and Frutiger
Design and illustration: David Coventon
Printed in China by Imago

ISBN: 1905403011

The Wit and Wisdom of Football

Compiled by Guy Lloyd,

a man of taste and humour, 2004.

AURA BOOKS

Contents

Boardroom B*ll*cks

Lies and Litigation 005

Of course I am prepared to bury the hatchet – right in the back of Sam Longson's head. **Brian Clough on not kissing and making up with his former chairman at Derby.**

What's the difference is between three minutes to three and five o'clock? I'm not sure. **Lincoln chairman John Reames puts the football to the back of his mind.**

We haven't fallen out. You can't fall out with somebody you never talk to. **Keegan on Newcastle chairman Sir John Hall.**

I'd like to thank Stan for his interest but we won't be taking it seriously. **Chairman Geoffrey Richmond politely declines Stan Collymore's application to become Bradford City's manager.**

The only reason David won't be manager of Leeds will be if he walks out because he and I are in this together. **Peter Ridsdale, Leeds chairman, six weeks before sacking O'Leary.** *FourFourTwo* Sept 02

In many ways he's an absolute ignorant pig, but he does care about the club.
Barnet manager Barry Fry on Stan Flashman, the club's ticket-touting chairman.

He couldn't run a kebab shop.
Millwall chairman Theo Paphitis on Football League chief executive David Burns.

We spoke about it really and out of it came the fact that we wouldn't speak about it. **Terry Venables on discussions about his future with 'Boro chairman Steve Gibson.**

We will not miss him. He can't head the ball and he rarely passes the ball more than three metres. **Real Madrid president, Florentino Perez, as Claude Makele departs for Stamford Bridge.**
Independent quotes of the year

They want us to be a nodding dog in the back of their car. **The PFA's Gordon Taylor bemoans the attitude of the Premier League.**

I will close Hull City down if I don't get proper backing from the club and supporters, and those who don't like it can get stuffed. **Proprietor David Lloyd.**

I don't believe evil should triumph and he was an evil man. I did not grieve because I am not a hypocrite... he was full of bullshit, star-struck and up Glenn Hoddle's arse. **Chelsea chairman Ken Bates reflects on director Matthew Harding's fatal helicopter crash.**

Get lost, Abramovich. I think I speak for the rest of football. **Charlton chairman Martin Simons is peeved about Chelsea's interest in Scott Parker.** *Observer* 25/01/04

Our only regret is that Jack Walker invested in Blackburn, not us. **Darwen's chairwoman Kath Marah** *The Guardian* 23/08/03

The great thing about local rivalries is that when things are going pear-shaped, you can have a go at your neighbour. Step forward our good friends at Crippled Alice who took umbrage with our decision to part company with Mark.

Millwall chairman Theo Paphitis blasts Crystal Palace after they criticised their rival's sacking of manager Mark McGhee.

I'd rather die and have vultures eat my insides than share with Crystal Palace. **Wimbledon chairman Sam Hammam.**

There's a village somewhere that's missing a fool. **Paphitis again, this time slating Burnley boss Stan Ternent after claims of racism by Millwall fans.**

The ideal soccer board of directors should be made up of three men; two dead, and the other dying.
Tommy Docherty

Sport needs competition and interesting opponents, otherwise boredom sets in and nobody wants to come to the games any more. **Retiring UEFA chief executive, Gerhard Aigner, on concentration of power.** *Independent* 29/12/03

I have flown economy and haven't had a problem with it. It's good discipline. **Chairman Peter Hill-Wood relegates Arsenal's players after a pre-season trip to Austria.** *Independent* quotes of the year

Soccer is like vodka ten years ago. The public's going to have to be educated to it. **W.B Cutler, US soccer club chairman, on his plans to market the game in the States.**

The supporters don't matter as far as I'm concerned. They just pay their entrance fee. I don't care whether they come to Barnet or not... **The late Barnet chairman, Stan Flashman.**

If a Russian billionaire came in I would not only roll out the red carpet but I would hoist up the red flag. **Bob Murray, Sunderland chairman.** *Independent* 02/02/04

In a fairly dull kingdom there were two players who were perfectly happy, because they had firm contracts. However, due to a shortage of beans, the two players were dispatched to far-flung kingdoms to ply their trade with other clubs. **Start of programme notes from QPR chairman David Davies, February 2004.** *The Guardian* 28/02/04

They go in because they are football crazy, or football mad. You have to be bloody crackers to be a director of a football club anyway. Who'd pour money into football when you can earn 10% with it, maybe 20% with it?
Ex-Palace chairman Arthur Wait.

OK, they cost us £20 a month to hire, but they were in the club colours of blue and yellow.
Peter Ridsdale justifies the hire of tropical fish to decorate his office.

That's a matter between directors and club. Listen, lad, I wouldn't even tell the wife. Stafford Heginbotham, ex-Bradford City chairman, on how much he had invested.

I got calls from Italy last summer and one agent offered me Gabriel Batistuta. He told me 'Batistuta wants to come to Chelsea.' I said 'I'm sure he does, but we've stopped signing pensioners.' Ken Bates wins another friend.

I never make forecasts, but whoever wins that game will win the Final. Ken Bates

I'm delighted for Claudio Ranieri that we beat Fulham in the FA Cup semi-final, as if we'd lost yesterday, it would have been a pity to sack him just after he'd signed a new contract. Ken Bates dispenses with the vote of confidence.

Supporters, shareholders, the press, the manager, nobody was saying don't do it. **Peter Ridsdale passes the buck for Leeds' financial fall from grace.** *Observer Sport magazine,* March 2004

The first thing I read now in the *Telegraph* is the obituaries. If I'm not in it, I have a good day. **Wolves chairman Jack Hayward looks on the bright side of life.** *The Guardian* 11/8/03

I'd like to finish on page one of Ceefax. **Chairman Jack Hayward on Wolves Premiership ambitions, August 2003.** *The Guardian* 11/8/03

Every fan you ask will say he wants to see lively, open football. But what the fan really wants to see is his team win. **Dennis Hill-Wood, Arsenal director.**

I haven't felt this bad since I killed a man.
Uri Geller, Exeter director and former Israeli soldier, on his team's
relegation to the Conference. *Independent* quotes of the year

Sacking a manager is as big an event in my life as drinking a glass of beer. I'd hire twenty managers a year if I wanted to, 100 if necessary. President of Atletico Madrid, Jesus Gil.

Cardiff are a substantially bigger club than Leeds. Chairman Sam Hamman pours oil before an FA Cup Tie.

I have a clear message to Sir Alex and anyone else who is interested: "read my lips, Louis Saha is not for sale."
Fulham chairman Mohammed Al Fayed lays it on the line, 6th January 2004, a couple of weeks before Saha left for Old Trafford. *The Guardian* 07/01/04

In ten years' time this club will be in the Premier League.
Michael Knighton in 1992, on buying Carlisle United. They dropped into the Conference in 2004.

Newcastle girls are all dogs. England is full of them.

Newcastle director Freddie Shepherd unwittingly spills the beans to an undercover tabloid hack.

Shearer's boring. We call him Mary Poppins. He never gets into trouble.

Freddie Shepherd... again... to the same journalist.

Our fans like people like Keith Gillespie – they relate to people who like to have a drink and get into trouble. Newcastle chairman Douglas Hall.

We have made an undertaking to Arsene Wenger and his family not to name our new coach. **Arsenal chairman Peter Hill-Wood.**

Tell the Kraut to get his ass up front. We don't pay a million for a guy to hang around in defence. **A New York Cosmos executive questions Franz Beckenbauer's position.**

Let the women play in more feminine clothes, like they do in volleyball. They could, for example, have tighter shorts. Female players are pretty, if you excuse me for saying so… **FIFA president Sepp Blatter.** *The Guardian* 16/01/04

My job will be to make sure that he scores more goals than own goals. **Publicist Max Clifford on his new client, Mohammed Al Fayed.**

The rumours are all driving us mad. Paul is staying with us. I wish people would leave it alone. Paul's totally committed to the club. **Plymouth chairman Paul Stapleton, two days before manager Paul Sturrock left for Southampton.** *Observer* 07/03/04

I didn't buy Manchester United so why should I buy Arsenal? We'll thrash them all at the Manor. Robert Maxwell blusters about Oxford United.

Me and Joe are so close, we will continue living in the same underpants. **Ex-Wimbledon chairman Sam Hammam talks pants.**

I'm leaving the asylum to the lunatics. Keith Harris ends his tenure as Football League chairman.

If I had a son I'd prefer he went to war than play soccer. There are terrible battles in soccer, worse than war itself. Real Madrid president Santiago Bernabeu, 1964.

It is the board's view that in spite of recent results, the team's performance has failed to live up to the high standard of football entertainment expected of Manchester United.
Statement from Manchester United dismissing manager Dave Sexton in 1981.
The team has just won its seventh game in a row.

Maxwell Chairman? We may as well have Max Wall. Derby fanzine *The Sheep*.

Once it was lucky Arsenal. Then it was boring Arsenal, but now we've got a real problem because we're in danger of being liked. Arsenal chairman Peter Hill-Wood on the flair of late '90s Arsenal.

As we say in the Conference, they didn't like it when we got inside their pants. I've never seen Shearer out of his pram like that. He didn't like it when we wouldn't let them play.

Victor Green, Stevenage chairman, after holding Newcastle in an FA Cup tie.

What's Stan doing? It would be fair to say that nobody at Bradford City has a clue.

Chairman Geoffrey Richmond admits Stan Collymore has gone a.w.o.l.

If I had to choose between the Israelis or Tony Blair to protect me, then Israel wins every time. Ken Bates remains unimpressed by some Chelsea players' refusal to fly to Tel Aviv for a UEFA Cup Tie.

I have a gun and a licence and I wouldn't mind blowing their brains out. **Nuremberg president Adolf Roth reacts badly to his team's 2-1 defeat to Lubeck.** *Observer* 12/10/03

We play at Wembley stadium, not the London Palladium. England selector's reason for not picking the 'clown prince' Len Shackleton.

Carreras, Santi and Otero are no good. They can die. I mean it: some of the players don't deserve to live. Atletico Madrid president Jesus Gil.

A piece of bread, and a very sensitive one. Self-portrait by Atletico Madrid supremo Jesus Gil *Observer* 2003

There is a psychological value…
you can imagine when the players of
an opposition team go out knowing
that Darth Vader is watching them.

Exeter chairman Uri Geller reacting to Dave Prowse becoming an honourary director.
Independent **quotes of the year**

I liken the current situation to that
of the Starship Enterprise. The
shields are up and the Klingons
are shooting at us and every time
they land a punch they are sapping
our power… **Southampton chairman Rupert Lowe proves**
Gordon Strachan wasn't the only eccentric at
St. Mary's. *Observer* 15/02/04

You should see his boots. They're like something you hang from your car mirror. **Middlesbrough chairman Steve Gibson marvels at the size of Juninho's feet.** *The Guardian* 27/02/04

I've often looked at other people getting involved in games like that and thought 'What a prat'. Perhaps I enjoyed it a little more than I should have but I was wrapped up in the occasion. **Middlesbrough chairman Steve Gibson after celebrating his club's first major trophy, the Carling Cup, in 2004.** *The Guardian* 01/03/04

I've got a gut feeling in my stomach…
Alan Sugar passes his anatomy test.

I parted on good terms with Luca Vialli. As he left the room and I led him to the door, we departed with the usual Italian formalities of a bear-hug and a kiss. **Ken Bates attempts to prove that not everybody hated him.**

I can't ever leave this club. I was born 300 yards from Molineux. The only way I'll leave this place is in a coffin. **Jack Hayward declares undying allegiance to Wolves.**

Even Jesus Christ suffered only one Pontius Pilate.
I had a whole team of them. **Ken Bates resigns in a huff from the company contracted to rebuild Wembley.**

He has left the Theatre of Dreams for the Team of Dreams. **Real Madrid president Florentino Perez welcomes David Beckham.**

The World Cup, believe it or not, was brought to my house and I held it in my hands and closed my eyes, and I energized it for England. To be very honest with you, I even managed to bend it ever so slightly. **Uri Geller. Course you did, Uri.**

Win or die. **Mussolini's pre-match telegram before the 1938 World Cup Final had the desired effect. Italy won.**

Lombardo speaks much better English than what people realise. Ex-Palace chairman Mark Goldberg.

David Beckham

He has transcended the classic footballing context. He is an integral part of show business. But unlike Anna Kournikova, he does the business on the pitch. **Marcel Desailly on David Beckham.** *Times,* 31/12/03

He can't kick with his left foot. He doesn't score many goals. He can't head a ball. And he can't tackle. Apart from that he's all right. **George Best,** *Observer*

Beckham is more of a pop star than a footballer. **Pele is not impressed by Beckham** *The Guardian* 01/09/03

It's not easy when someone pulls your ponytail. **David Beckham on provocation.** *Independent* **quotes of the year**

Beckham will take the free kick and he's a world class bender. **German commentary during the 2002 World Cup finals.**

This Gaultier-saronged, Posh Spiced, Cooled Britannia, look-at-me, what-a-lad, loadsamoney, sex-and-shopping, fame-schooled, daytime-TV, over-coiffed twerp, did not, of course, mean any harm.

The Daily Telegraph has a hissy fit about Beckham's sending-off at France '98.

I definitely want Brooklyn to be christened, but I don't know into what religion yet.

I am always going to be ten times more famous than David Beckham. Lennox Lewis, *Independent* quotes of the year

I went for the gaffer. I don't know if I've ever lost control like that before. Suddenly it was like some mad scene out of a gangster movie. **Beckham bites back after Fergie's flying boot.**

I'm sorry David. I didn't mean to do that. An apology! From Fergie!!!

Alex Ferguson is the best manager I've ever had at this level. Well, he's the only manager I've ever had at this level. **Beckham whilst at Manchester United.**

He's absolutely the most gorgeous, gorgeous, gorgeous person. I mean, he's sheer and utter heaven. **Actress Stephanie Beacham after meeting David Beckham on Parkinson.** *Independent* **quotes of the year**

Well, I can play in the centre, on the right and occasionally on the left side. **On being asked whether he was a volatile player.**

When I heard about the death threat on Brooklyn I had sympathy for David. I hate him because he plays for Manchester United but that threat was below the belt.

Oasis frontman Liam Gallagher sympathises with the price of fame.

Becks hasn't changed since I've known him. He's always been a flash Cockney git.

Ryan Giggs *Independent* quotes of the year

My parents have always been there for me, ever since I was about seven.

I don't understand the rules of football but there are some lovely songs they sing about me. **Mrs Beckham does sarcasm.**

Never, never, never, never.
Nothing, never, never, never.
Not now. Not ever.

**Real Madrid president, Florentino Perez, on
whether the club would sign David Beckham.**
Independent quotes of the year

At least he won't be signing for Real Madrid.

Sky's Martin Tyler comments on Beckham's end-of-season injury.
Independent quotes of the year

My dad always told me to keep my mouth shut.
Now I've realised I've reached the stage where
I must learn to do it in big tournaments. I know
I'll never be sent off playing for England.

David Beckham, shortly before France '98.

Without being too hard on David,
he cost us the match. **Ian Wright on that Beckham sending-
off against Argentina.**

If I say Beckham is a "pretty boy", suddenly they say I'm gay, or that Beckham's gay. It's not like that. Nobody's gay! Diego Maradona plays it straight. *Observer* 08/02/04

If the spit had hit me on the head I wouldn't have been annoyed but it hit the crescent and the star on my Turkey shirt. Turkey's Alpay claims that Beckham spat at him during a Euro 2004 qualifier. *Independent* quotes of the year

I can only speak for myself, but I miss him as a man, as a guy in the dressing room and as a player on the pitch. It was great to play alongside him. Ruud van Nistelrooy laments Becks' departure from Old Trafford.

In the Ivy they don't let anyone ask for autographs. I know this because Michael Jordan was in there one night and I wasn't able to get his signature.

Money, Money, Money:

I've still one or two ambitions left. Number one is to make £50,000 by the time I'm 25, and number two is to own a chain of shops and, who knows, eventually to become a millionaire. **George Best maps out the future, 1967.**

We lived the dream.

Ex-Leeds chairman Peter Ridsdale, who left the club £80m in debt.
Independent quotes of the year

It's like an oil tanker that's heading for the rocks… the trouble with oil tankers is they're two miles long and they don't turn round in two minutes. **Leeds chairman John McKenzie on picking up the financial pieces at Elland Road.**

The lenders wanted to go up to £75m but we closed on £60m.
Broker Steven Schechter on how he secured Leeds' fateful loan, the biggest-ever for a British football club, in 2001. *Observer Sport magazine,* March 2004

If they had listened to me the supporters would be sitting in a 70,000-seater stadium in Dublin and in the Premiership.
Former Wimbledon boss Joe Kinnear tells the board so.

I'll give him a fresh start if he's prepared to take a thousand a week.
Darlington chairman George Reynolds muses on signing Paul Gascoigne.

We are standing in a one-way alley with bullets flying all around us.
John Smith, co-chairman at Bury, spells out his club's financial position.

If it is a case of losing 10,000 season tickets versus the £9m we have just generated from Jonathan Woodgate, there is no discussion.
Leeds chairman Peter Ridsdale endears himself to supporters...not. *Times*, 31/12/03

He has been very well paid for his time at the club. It's not as if he's going to end up in a bedsit in Gipton.
Simon Jose, co-founder of Leeds United Independent Fans' Association, on Peter Ridsdale. *Times*, 31/12/03

It wasn't the Leeds thing to do at all. Leeds is built on good, solid Jewish money. And a lot of good, solid Jewish people are lamenting what Peter Ridsdale did. Leeds local Martin Pickles. *The Guardian* 10/02/04

To be perfectly blunt, the introduction of the Bosman ruling was a disaster for sport and especially for football.

Gerhard Aigner, former UEFA chief executive. *The Guardian* 07/01/04

With Ravanelli and Emerson, perhaps their brains really were in their boots and their hearts in their wallets. Middlesbrough chairman Steve Gibson.

I have spent some time with some tough cookies over the years, Mrs Thatcher and Saddam Hussein to name but two. But when it comes to ruthlessness in defence of his own interests, Ken Bates leaves them all behind. David Mellor

I raised the matter [of top-rate season tickets at £1,000] with Ken Bates the other day. He just replied "You can afford it". This attitude is becoming all too evident in football. Tony Banks, Chelsea fan and ex-Minister for Sport.

I think the motive of a club is to earn more money and if it meant it was annoying or inconvenient to other home fans, I think that is secondary to a club's policy of earning extra revenue. **Harvey Harris of a Spurs's supporters action group.**

In 2007, £75 million will be no more than the price of a decent left-back. **Ken Bates, then Chelsea chairman, brushes off the size of the club's debt.**

The listening bank refused to listen and the bank which likes to say yes said no. **Hartlepool chairman Garry Gibson contemplates a winding-up order from the inland revenue.**

The local pubs aren't happy that there's 25,000 and not 48,000 in the ground. And then there's the nearby strip club and the strippers aren't too happy either. It's bad for top totty and the lap-dancing club has closed.

Sunderland chairman Bob Murray laments the post-relegation recession.
Nuts

I think what's going on is sad and disappointing because everyone that's helped give the club history and tradition is being sold down the river. **Ex-Wimbledon hero Dave Beasant laments the current state of the Dons.** *Observer* 08/02/04

I've had enough. As soon as I get home, I'm going to buy that club. I'm going to walk in and say "You, f**k off. You, f**k off. You, make me a cup of tea. You, f**k off.

Noel Gallagher muses whether the Oasis school of diplomacy will work at Manchester City.

Maxwell, please buy me.

Israeli car sticker after Robert Maxwell's interest in buying two Jerusalem football clubs.

It is not easy to change a culture in which people are used to hiding things. They might not have anything to hide but the tendency is to secrecy. **Kate Barker, chair of the the FA's Finance Advisory Committee, February 2004.** *The Guardian* 09/02/04

I believe that the introduction of big money to English football has had side effects. There is more violence. But these problems, which arise out of the new professional attitude of the players, are rather like those of the spirited young horse which needs controlling firmly. **Jimmy Hill reflects on the abolition of the maximum wage, 1967.**

We needed someone with deeper pockets than I've got. **Ken Bates recognises the buying power of new owner Roman Abramovich.**

Roman Abramovich has parked his Russian tank in our front garden and is firing £50 notes at us. **Arsenal director David Dein gets envious.**

There's a prosperous sound about twenty pounds a week. It rolls off the tongue, but it doesn't roll into the pockets of every player.
Brian Clough, 1958.

He's just throwing money in the wind, and that has never worked.
Johnny Giles on Abramovich's spending spree.

It makes the house that Jack built at Blackburn look like a bungalow.
Henk Potts, financial analyst, on Roman Abramovich's spending at Chelsea. *Independent* quotes of the year

I'm like a kid in a sweet shop.
Claudio Ranieri likes his new lolly. *The Guardian* 23/08/03

Maybe there is someone in the world who can imitate my voice and has my cheque book, as he buys players every day.
Arsene Wenger scoffs at the latest transfer rumours. *Nuts*

Why leave a club that is two quid in debt and go to a club that is £80m in debt?

Norwich manager Nigel Worthington dismisses talk that he is bound for Leeds. *Independent* quotes of the year

I think these foreign coaches have been blown up out of proportion. Let's see them at Chester, Darlington and Walsall with no money and see how they get on there. Peter Reid flies the flag.

You can spend £2m and find the player can not trap the ball. Graham Taylor on the inflated transfer market, 2001.

Money comes in at the top end and goes straight to the players. Then, when a player leaves, he'll blame the club and say he's sorry to go because he loves the place. Well it's crap. They want to move for a better deal and more money. It's just greed. On his way out, the player will probably ask for a loyalty bonus. Dave Bassett hits the nail on the head.

Celtic's support is the greatest asset… when you start talking about money, it is the supporters that put the money into the club. Martin O'Neill points out where the real wealth lies.

Only two clubs could buy him: Real Madrid and Chelsea. Everton manager David Moyes values Wayne Rooney *Times* 23/02/04

I can understand him being a little sad because his team were clearly dominated by a team who have maybe 10% of his budget. Porto coach Jose Mourinho digs after Alex Ferguson refused to shake hands after United's Champions League defeat. *The Guardian* 26/02/04

I cannot feed my child on glory.
Paolo Rossi during his pay dispute with Juventus.

Four years' work. A million pounds spent, and what did we get? Two free kicks. A Brazilian journalist berates the standard of refereeing at the 1966 World Cup as his country are literally booted out of the competition.

Any small boy, anyone who kicks a ball owns a piece of the action. Everybody enjoys the exaggeration and romance of a sporting story, but deliberate lying and cheating for profit is something else.
Danny Blanchflower, speaking in 1968, on power, corruption and money.

We bring in the crowds, it's an entertainment, and we're vastly underpaid, footballers, for the entertainment we provide. Stan Bowles

People have been making money out of me.
Don Revie answers criticism of greed, after he left England to take a coaching job in Saudi Arabia.

Two months ago he was over the moon, now he's asking for it. Juventus' official with his own take on Paolo Rossi's pay demands.

I, who have had the most privileged of lives, the most carefree of existences for nearly twenty years, have managed to get myself painted as a living saint for keeping my promise to myself. **Niall Quinn's take, in his autobiography, on his donation of a £1m testimonial gate to charity.**

I want to buy Buckingham Palace but…

Arsene Wenger, on news that Barcelona had declared an interest in Thierry Henry.
The Guardian 24/02/04

No money in the world can buy a white England shirt.

Alan Shearer reveals his ignorance of merchandising.

On the last day of the 1995/96 season… the City souvenir shop discovered it had run out of the letters 'K' and 'Z'.

Manchester City fail to cash in on the sudden popularity of Georgi Kinkladze.
Manchester United Ruined my Life by Colin Shindler, Headline, 1998.

I found love in my life at first sight – with Leeds it's the same. I don't want to look at any other club. I love this country and this city! I wake up happy.

Roque Junior. Three months later a cash-strapped Leeds released him.
Observer 25/01/04

When my career ends, I cannot go the baker and say "I'm Johann Cruyff, give me some bread".

Cruyff on the need to keep earning bread. *Brilliant Orange*, Bloomsbury, 2000

Listen, for the next three years while I am in Spain, I am not a man. I am not a football player. I am an industry.

Johann Cruyff after signing a $1m contract with Barcelona, 1973.

When I was a lad, I took nothing for granted, the air I breathed or even a scrap of bread. Now you can offer a boy the world and he'll probably turn his nose up.

Bill Shankly despairs of the nation's youth.

I don't know how much it is. My father told me that when you're working, don't stop to count your money.

Pele in 1974, on being asked how much he was worth.

Everybody wants to speak to me now I've got money.

Ken Bates on the power of Abramovich.

Yeah. I have been offered money to sign somebody and there's not a manager in the country who would tell you different. If they did they'd be lying. Harry Redknapp

It's costing me a fortune, because as well as the fares I'm arriving late for training a few times. We have a deal where anyone who is late has to pay £50, so I've already written a cheque for £1,500 to see me through the season. **Paul Merson on playing for Middlesbrough and living in Hertfordshire.**

Don't know much about the game. Don't even like it much. What's that got to do with it? My business is selling people – makes no difference what they do. **Players' agent Eric Hall reveals his true love.**

The terrible thing about my job is that players get 80% of my earnings. **Agent Eric Hall inflates his importance... again.**

It may be good enough for the homeless but not for an international striker. **Pierre van Hooijdonk's rejection of a £7,000 per week pay rise.** *Observer Sport Monthly*

Football is a street where every second building is a last-chance saloon.
The Sunday Times' **David Walsh waxes all lyrical.**

When you look at other sports, like golf, the players earn a lot more money without running around. I wish I had that little cart to take me to the corner kicks. **Thierry Henry.** *Times,* 31/12/03

Pulling down your shorts on a football field is a) against our regulations because it is ungentlemanly conduct, and b) it is also against the FIFA regulation which stipulates that footballers are barred from using their bodies or undergarments beneath their kit as advertisement boards. **FA spokesman Adrian Bevington warns Scarborough players not to exploit too many commercial opportunities during their FA Cup tie against Chelsea.** *The Guardian* 23/01/04

You couldn't buy him today. I would say that he is the finest player that I ever saw in my life. For fifty games a season I would have Finney in my team before Pele, Cruyff and Di Stefano.
Tommy Docherty on Tom Finney.

Football in the 1970s is very rewarding financially and can provide the opportunity to travel to almost any country in the world.
Don Revie, shortly before walking out of the England job to take up a lucrative coaching post in Saudi Arabia.

Some people tell me that we professional players are soccer slaves. Well, if this is slavery, give me a life sentence. Bobby Charlton on the maximum wage, 1960.

If I never kicked another ball I could afford to live well for the rest of my life. It is a comforting thought for a man only twenty-four years old. Pele in 1965.

I can play football at my level for £500 a month, because I love it so much.
Marcel Desailly has his fingers crossed, 2003.

Players who play to lose are worse than bank robbers.
Bill Shankly

The whole problem with Hillsborough seems to be it was the fans who suffered and died and they haven't got any benefits out of Hillsborough at all, and so many other people have.
Sheila Spiers of the Football Supporters' Association.

He spat on Russia by buying Chelsea. He abandoned our teams which need support.
Mayor of Moscow Yuri Lushnov on Roman Abramovich.
Independent quotes of the year

Any soccer club that pays income tax at the end its financial year, I would fine them exactly the same amounts on the grounds that they were guilty of bad management. Soccer can not afford to lose a penny that comes into the game, let alone pay it out in income tax. Brian Clough, 1973.

I believe Wembley is the next Millennium Dome. There will be a lot of tears if they continue this project.

Villa Chairman Doug Ellis.

If Pele was on the market today for £100m, then we'd maybe go for him but we won't pay £30m for Joe Nobody. Chelsea's acting chief executive Paul Smith reveals the club's spending plans. *The Guardian* 12/03

I'm going to have to listen for offers for all my players – and the club cat, Benny, who is pissed off because there are no mice to catch because they have all died of starvation. John McGrath, Halifax manager, in 1992.

He's only selling me so he'll look good to the fans.

Leeds keeper Paul Robinson criticises chairman John McKenzie's decision to sell him, only to remain at Elland Road when his proposed move to Villa fell through.

How can you sympathise with a club which had a perfectly good stadium seven years ago but sold it to Toys R Us? **Brighton fan Paul Millmore.** *Daily Telegraph* 26/02/04

Northampton are currently making payments to four managers but not paying any bills. **Terry Fenwick comments on a 48-day tenure as the Cobblers' manager.**

I'm aware of the situation. There's not £10m to spend. There's not even 10p. **Tony Adams's verdict on Wycombe's finances** *The Guardian* 10/11/03

I am here to earn big money at Tottenham and to meet English girls. **Spurs' new signing Moussa Saib sets out his priorities.**

If I wanted to sign a Madrid player my first call would be to the club, not the newspapers. I expect a bit more class from Real Madrid. **Arsene Wenger, after Real's interest in Thierry Henry is made public.** *Independent* 14/02/04

It spends money it hasn't got on players who aren't worth it. What kind of business is that? A bankrupt one is the answer.

Michael Parkinson despairs of football's finances.

Brian Clough

Sky are overkilling it because they're even boring me, and I'm a fanatic.

Brian Clough *Observer* 2003

I've seen big men hide in corridors to avoid him. He can make you feel desperate for his approval.

Martin O'Neill on Brian Clough.

I think Arsene Wenger should have been fined several times over for his team's behaviour – forty sendings-off in his first five years as manager is nothing short of a disgrace.

The only person certain of boarding the coach for the Littlewoods Cup Final is Albert Kershaw, and he'll be driving it.

Brian Clough keeps his team-sheet close to his chest.

If the BBC ran a Crap Decision of the Month competition on Match of the Day, I'd walk it. Humble offerings from Brian Clough on Forest's relegation in 1993.

When he finished playing he went into the licensed trade and became the only landlord I know who was bigger and wider than his own pub. Brian Clough on former centre-half Larry Lloyd.

God gave you intelligence, skill, agility and the best passing ability in the game. What God didn't give you was six studs to wrap around someone else's knee. Brian Clough to Leeds' Johnny Giles.

My wife said to me in bed, "God, your feet are cold." I said, "You can call me Brian in bed, dear." Pillow talk from Clough

When I was admitted to the heart unit, somebody sent me a 'get well' telegram that said "we didn't even know you had one".

Brazil, the favourites – if they are the favourites, which they are… Ol' Big Head gets tongue-tied.

I don't know anybody in a responsible position, or your average working man, who doesn't have a drink, but I was drinking far in excess of what I should have been doing. I had become dependent. Brian Clough comes clean in his autobiography.

It's those bums on the sports pages I hate most. Brian Clough on the press.

He's not actually a very good player but he's got a lovely smile that brightens up Monday mornings. **Brian Clough considers re-signing Neil Webb.**

If you come any closer to me, we might as well get into the same pair of shorts and save a few bob on laundry. **Brian Clough, the player, to Doncaster's Charlie Williams.**

But how I would love to have been Ali. You can't be better than the best, greater than the greatest, and who wouldn't want to be called that and deserve it. Certainly not a conceited, self-opinionated beggar like me. **Brian Clough admits that there is someone bigger than him.**

I wouldn't say I was the best manager in the business, but I was in the top one.

Look at your players prior to the coach leaving and count the hearts. If there are less than five, don't bother setting off. A team's no good without courage. **Harry Storer, a mentor of Brian Clough, offers sound advice.**

He didn't look anything like a professional athlete when I first clapped eyes on him. In fact, there were times when he barely resembled a member of the human race. **Clough on former Forest winger John Robertson.**

I'm a bighead, not a figurehead.

In this business, you've got to be a dictator or you haven't got a chance.

Like all the great dictators, from de Gaulle to Thatcher, he stayed on a little too long. *Gazzetta dello Sport,* Italy's leading sports paper, on Brian Clough.

Coaching is for kids. If a player can't trap a ball and pass it by the time he's in the team, he shouldn't be there in the first place. I told Roy McFarland to go and get his bloody hair cut – that's coaching at this level.

When UEFA get in their stride, they make the FA look like kindergarten material.

One of the best socialists I've ever met.

Former Labour Party leader Michael Foot on Brian Clough.

Women run everything. The only thing I've done within my house in the last twenty years is recognise Angola as an independent state. Brian Clough admits he finally defers to someone.

I had a walk along the River Trent today. As you know, it's my normal practice to walk on it. On being made a freeman of Nottingham, Brian Clough address the civic reception in his honour.

Manager-speak

The whole thing was unreal, like a freak of nature.

Alf Ramsey on surrendering a two-goal lead to Germany, which spelled England's exit from the 1970 World Cup.

I think everyone in the stadium went home happy, except all those people in Romania.

England manager Ron Greenwood after a World Cup qualifier in Romania.

When you are 4-0 up, you should never lose 7-1.

Southampton manager Lawrie McMenemy is shell-shocked after a pasting at Watford.

Bryan Robson. Well, he does what he does and his future is in the future. Ron Greenwood turns astrologer.

There's a rat in the camp trying to throw a spanner in the works.

Brighton boss Chris Cattlin in metaphor madness.

Today's top players only want to play in London or for Manchester United. That's what happened when I tried to sign Alan Shearer and he went to Blackburn. Graeme Souness

We have faced African teams, we have faced English teams – so we are ready to face Scotland because we know what their play will be like. **Brazilian coach Mario Zagallo flunks the geography test before the 1998 World Cup curtain-raiser against Scotland.**

The lads ran their socks into the ground.
Alex Ferguson

We can't behave like crocodiles and cry over spilled milk and broken eggs.
Italian coach Giovanni Trappatoni loses it in translation.

It was a game we should have won. We lost it because we thought we were going to win it. But, then again, I thought there was no way we were going to get a result there. **Jack Charlton**

There is great harmonium in the dressing room.
Sir Alf Ramsey

If in winning we could only draw we would be fine.
Jack Charlton

It would be a nice scalp for Scunthorpe to put Wimbledon on our bottoms.
Dave Bassett

Chester made it hard for us by having two players sent off.

John Docherty

I'm definitely maybe going to play Sturrock.
Dundee United boss Jim McLean.

The one thing I didn't expect is the way we didn't play. George Graham

You weigh up the pros and cons and try to put them into chronological order. Dave Bassett

Davor has a left leg and a nose in the box.
Arsene Wenger on the anatomy of striker Davor Suker.

I don't read everything I read in the press.
Dave Jones

David [Johnson] has scored 62 goals in 148 games for Ipswich and those statistics tell me that he plays games and scores goals. **David Platt**

The run of the ball is not in our court at the moment.
Phil Neal

I'm not superstitious or anything like that, but I just hope we'll play our best and put it in the lap of the gods. **Terry Neill**

At the end of the day, it's all about what's on the shelf at the end of the year. **Steve Coppell proves that his time at university wasn't wasted.**

I'm not going to make it a target but it's something to aim for.
Steve Coppell

Being given chances and not taking them, that's what life is all about.
Ron Greenwood

We have to roll up our sleeves and get our knees dirty. Howard Wilkinson

He's gone in there with studs up and has cut someone in half, but I don't want to criticise him. John Gregory

If Ricardo Gardner should have been sent off, there should have been four players sent off for each side. So the match should have ended up six against six. Sam Allardyce

Playing another side could be an omen, but I don't believe in omens.
George Graham

That was clearly a tackle aimed at getting revenge, or maybe it was just out-and-out retribution.

Joe Royle

Pele had nearly everything. Maradona has everything. He works harder, does more and is more skillful. Trouble is that he'll be remembered for another reason. He bends the rules to suit himself. **Sir Alf Ramsey**

Why not? Hopefully the boss will be around for a few more years but yeah, it has crossed my mind. **Roy Keane on the manager's job at Old Trafford.** *Independent* 29/12/03

At the end of the day, the Arsenal fans demand that we put eleven players on the pitch. **Don Howe**

I, Tinkerman, will not change.
Claudio Ranieri delights in his alias *The Guardian* 23/08/03

We have a one-sided window looking over the players' gym from our physio room. It means we can keep an eye on them… Bryan Robson at Middlesbrough.

I've always loved left-footed players. There's something about them that is very sexy. John Gregory

There is no place for a gay in my team. And I could easily spot one if he tried to get into my team. Gays are no good and can not be role models for our youth. Croatian coach Otto Baric *Observer* 25/01/04

He's not a tackler. I've told him don't bother tackling because you can't tackle. I'm fed up saying that to him. When he does go into tackles he doesn't know how to do it and ends up getting a booking. Alex Ferguson spots a flaw in Cantona's game.

Eric likes to do what he likes, when he likes, because he likes it – and then f**k off. We'd all want a bit of that. Howard Wilkinson on the perils of dealing with Cantona.

It's the only stadium in the world I've ever been in that's absolutely buzzing with atmosphere when it's empty and there isn't a soul inside.
Tommy Docherty on Old Trafford.

Football is war.
Former Holland coach Rinus Michels. *Brilliant Orange:*

Every defeat is a victory in itself.
Colombia manager Francisco Maturana looks on the bright side.

Attilio Lombardo is starting to pick up a bit of English on the training ground. The first word he learned was wanker.
Steve Coppell on the rarefied atmosphere at Crystal Palace.

I just panicked.
Graham Taylor's explanation for signing Ian Ormondroyd for Aston Villa.

Charlie Nicholas's mouth is bigger than his head. He said that Maurice Malpas stamped on Jean-Marc Boco's chest, when in fact he stamped on his stomach.
Dundee United manager Tommy McLean.

John, you're immortal.
Bill Shankly to Jock Stein after Celtic's 1967 European Cup triumph.

I thought my team talk must have lost something in translation when we were a goal down in under a minute and turned round three goals behind.

Palace's Attilio Lombardo on the perils of being a non-English speaking manager.

Ian Marshall has been fantastic for us. When he's fit, he's superb. It's just that he's never fit. Martin O'Neill

If you are that full of yourself, as Arsenal are, it can come back to haunt you. Alex Ferguson on Arsenal's eight-point lead in the Premiership. *Independent* quotes of the year

A lot of people seem to think I'm a slippery cockney boy with a few jokes. It has taken one of the biggest clubs in the world to acknowledge what I can really do – coach. Terry Venables on his managership of Barcelona.

This is normal. When we win, Mr Abramovich wins. When Chelsea lose, Ranieri loses.

Claudio comments on press speculation about his job. *Independent* 29/12/03

Yee-hah! I've looked like I've had a coat hanger in my mouth ever since. **Mick McCarthy is clearly delighted to be appointed manager of Sunderland.**

When I don't put him in the squad my mother, who's 84, asks "why isn't Damien playing?" She kills me about it and that s true. **Chelsea boss Claudio Ranieri reveals his mother's admiration for Damien Duff.** *Independent* 27/12/03

A football team is like a beautiful woman. When you do not tell her so, she forgets to be beautiful. **Arsene Wenger**

I have been a fighter all my life but this one has beaten me. **Former Blackburn manager, Ray Harford, shortly before succumbing to lung cancer.** *Independent* quotes of the year

Bookings for getting stuck in are OK. Even the odd red card is all right, as long as it is for giving your all. I want my team to be horrible. I want opponents to hate playing us. **Dennis Wise sets out his stall as Millwall player-manager.**
Independent **quotes of the year**

I will calm down when I retire or die.
Martin O'Neill refuses to employ his reverse gear.

Statistics are like miniskirts. They give you good ideas but hide the most important things.
Hibs manager Ebbe Skovdahl.

He's fast, strong, sharp and skillful but otherwise he's useless. Norwich boss Ken Brown on Tony Woodcock.

I went to look at him playing for Wealdstone on a stinking night at Yeovil. After eight minutes he put in a thundering tackle and the Yeovil winger landed in my wife s lap. I said to her: 'That's it. I've seen enough. We're going home.' **Bobby Gould recalls the moment he decided to sign Stuart Pearce for Coventry.**

We wrote to Manchester United asking for permission to use their name and got a letter back from Sir Matt Busby telling us to go ahead. **Brian Askuez, manager of the other Manchester United in Gibraltar.**

There's only two teams in Liverpool; Liverpool and Liverpool reserves. **Bill Shankly**

I'm feeling like a drunk who hasn't got a drink. I'd never heard of Groundhog Day until recently but now I must go and see the film. **David Pleat, acting Spurs manager, intoxicated after a 4-4 draw against Leicester that saw his team blow a handsome lead for the second time in a few weeks. *Times* 23/02/04**

Squeaky-bum time. Alex Ferguson gives a soundbite on the end-of-season run-in.
The Guardian 23/02/04

It's a sorry state of affairs when the referee feels he's got equal billing with Eric Cantona. Eric came through his test, I'm not sure the referee did. Roy Evans on David Elleray after Eric Cantona's first game following a nine-month suspension.

It's 50-50. It's something that, at the moment, is in the fridge.

Real Madrid coach Carlos Queiroz talks gibberish when asked whether Viera would be leaving Arsenal. *Times*, 31/12/03

You've won it once, now you've got to win it again.
Sir Alf Ramsey famously exhorts England before extra-time in the 1966 World Cup Final. West Germany had equalised in the last minute.

No regrets, none at all. My only regret is that we went out on penalties. That's my only regret. But no, no regrets. Mick McCarthy is understandably tired and emotional after Ireland go out the 2002 World Cup to Spain.

I cannot tell you what is going to happen tomorrow – only today. And I can not even tell you what is going to happen today.

David Pleat on the precarious existence of being acting manager at Spurs. *Independent* 07/02/04

We threw our dice into the ring and turned up trumps. Bruce Rioch

To be really happy, we must throw our hearts over the bar and hope that our bodies will follow. Graham Taylor

In football, if you stand still you go backwards.

Peter Reid

There are two ways of getting the ball. One is from your team-mates and that's the only way. Terry Venables

The referee has a reputation of trying to make a name for himself. Graeme Souness

Shearer could be at 100% fitness
but not peak fitness. Graham Taylor

Give him his head and he'll
take it with both hands or feet.
Bobby Gould

We're going to start the
game at nil-nil and go out
and try and get some goals.
Bryan Robson

They had a dozen corners,
maybe twelve. I'm guessing.
Craig Brown

It's the only way we can lose,
irrespective of the result.
Graham Taylor

There are nil-nils
and nil-nils, and this
was nil-nil. John Sillett

If they hadn't scored,
we would have won.
Howard Wilkinson

In comparison, there's no comparison.
Ron Greenwood

If we can play like that every week, we'll get some level of consistency.
Alex Ferguson

And I honestly believe we can go all the way
to Wembley, unless somebody knocks us out.
Dave Bassett

In terms of the Richter scale, this was a force eight gale.
John Lyall

Out of nine red cards this season
we probably deserved half of them.
Arsene Wenger

I can count on the fingers of one
hand ten games where we've
caused our own downfall. **Joe Kinnear**

Certain people are for me, certain people are pro me.
Terry Venables

Outside of quality we had other qualities.
Bertie Mee

Even when you're dead, you must never allow yourself just to lie down and be buried. **Gordon Lee**

He's such an honest person it's untrue.
Brian Little

I like to think it's a case of crossing the 'i's and dotting the 't's. **Dave Bassett**

The important thing is, he shook hands with us over the phone. **Alan Ball**

Winning all the time is not necessarily good for the team.
John Toshack

I've seen them on television on a Sunday morning most days of the week. **Jack Charlton**

I just wonder what would have happened if the shirt had been on the other foot.

Mike Walker

Referees don't come down here with a particular flavoured shirt on.

Steve Coppell

Our first goal was pure textile.

John Lambie, legendary '70s manager of Partick Thistle.

It was not a mistake, it was a blunder.
Gerard Houllier

I just felt that the whole night, the conditions and taking everything into consideration and everything being equal, and everything is equal, we should have got something from the game, but we didn't. John Barnes loses it at Celtic.

It's a conflict of parallels.
Alex Ferguson

Inter have bought the finished article and there's no doubt he can keep improving.
Mick McCarthy

The mere fact that he's injured stops him getting injured again, if you know what I mean. Terry Venables

Paolo di Canio is capable of scoring the goal he scored.
Bryan Robson

His left foot is so good he could open a jar of pickles with it. John Gregory on the extraordinary powers of Steve Staunton.

We are Lego. Many bricks that fit together to make a smooth wall.

Poland manager Jerzy Engel before their first World Cup match in 2002. They lost.

You can't say my team aren't winners. They've proved that by finishing fourth, third and second in the last three years. Gerard Houllier

It was particularly pleasing that our goalscorers scored tonight. Alex Ferguson

I don't think the fans are too worried whether it's Tom Smith from Bury or Mussolini from Italy… as long as the team's doing well. David Pleat on Spurs' vacant managerial position.
The Guardian

We are a very good average team. Franz Beckenbauer is nearly modest.

We have to improve in two key areas: defence and attack.

Belgium national coach Robert Waseige on his team's performance in Euro 2000.

I never wanted this bloody job, but it looks like you're stuck with me.

Bob Paisley addresses the Liverpool players for the first time as manager. He led the club to thirteen major trophies, including three European Cups.

The last time I drove down here, I was in a tank liberating Italy.

Bob Paisley in Rome, en route to the 1977 European Cup Final.

It's nice for a bluenose to come here and win. I'm going to have a pint now and a gloat. Childhood Everton fan Dave Jones celebrates a Southampton victory at Anfield.

No complaints. I thought it was a soft penalty award anyway.

Liverpool manager Kenny Dalglish is magnanimous after John Aldridge's penalty miss costs them the 1988 Cup Final. *Observer Sport Monthly*

Age isn't important except on tombstones and birth certificates. He can still do the business. Tranmere manager John King after signing 35-year-old John Aldridge in 1991.

Ramon Vega went down like he was dead. I thought he had broken his leg but he only broke a tie-up. **Harry Redknapp**

These managers who buy players from videos, I find that impossible to believe. You never see the bit where the bloke falls over or turns to the manager and says "I ain't chasing that." **Joe Kinnear**

The problems at Wimbledon seem to be that the club has suffered a loss of complacency. **Joe Kinnear**

You can't give a team confidence. You can't put it in a pill, or a suppository. **Howard Wilkinson tries to explain Sunderland's capitulation in the Premier League.**

I understand the fans complaining. They wanted a big name and got me. **An unusually modest John Gregory on his appointment at Aston Villa.**

He was the heartbeat of the team in 1966. He was my right-hand man, my lieutenant on the field, a cool, calculating footballer I could trust with my life. **Sir Alf Ramsey pays tribute to Bobby Moore following his death from cancer in 1993.**

There should be a law against him. He knows what's happening 20 minutes before anyone else. **Jock Stein on Bobby Moore.**

I'd never allow myself to let myself call myself a coward. **Graham Taylor**

I admire the English mentality because you are so strong, so hard working. But we have talent.

Sven-Goran Eriksson on English football in 1991, after his Benfica side eliminated Arsenal from the European Cup.

That's not the worst reception I've ever had – did you ever see me as a player? **Bobby Gould reacts to a demonstration against him at the Hawthorns.**

Neil Lennon wasn't sent off for scoring a goal and that's what annoys me.
Martin O'Neill

When people tell me that fans want style and entertainment first I don't believe it. Fans want to win. Style's a bonus.
Lou Macari excuses his tactics as boss at Birmingham.

I'll try not to apologise too much for the game but I'm glad I got in for free.

Leicester manager Micky Adams defends a dire nil-nil at **Southampton**. *The Guardian* 08/01/04

One of the most important stadiums in the world.
Ruud Gullit on the prospect of playing at Plough Lane.
Observer Sport Monthly, 08/02/04

The ball hit a water sprinkler and shot high in the air. It was purely an instinctive reaction when he grabbed the ball as it flew over his head.
Scotland coach Andy Roxburgh defends Richard Gough's sending-off against Switzerland.

What I said to them at half-time would be unprintable on the radio. Gerry Francis

Down Among the Dead Men:

There's an old joke in football about the manager of a Fourth Division club, pushing out his humble team for a cup match against a big First Division club. 'Go out there lads and do your best' he exhorts them, 'so I can get enough money to replace you'.
Hunter Davies, from seminal football book The Glory Game.

I enjoyed myself playing for Scunthorpe – what more could you ask for? Kevin Keegan

Plenty of goals in Divisions Three and Four today; Darlington nil, Hereford nil.
BBC Radio 2 announcer.

Brentford reserves were involved in a nine-goal thriller when they beat Orient 4-3. Match report in the Ealing Gazette.

We learned a lot from United today, including how to count. Shrewsbury boss Kevin Ratcliffe laments an 8-1 pre-season hammering by Manchester United.

Chesterfield 1 Chester 1 – another score draw in the local derby. Des Lynam

It's now 4–3 to Oldham, the goals are going in like dominoes.
Over-excited report from Manchester's Piccadilly Radio.

I've lost count of how many corners there have been. Lincoln have one and Crystal Palace seventeen.
Ron Jones, Radio 5 Live.

When you re down, you Palace fans, the fickle finger of fate rarely smiles on you.
Jonathan Pearce

I set aside everything I learned under Arsene Wenger. It's a complete waste of time at this level. They just can't take a lot of information on board. Wycombe manager Tony Adams questions the tactical nous of his team.

Some of our players have got no brains, so I've given them the day off tomorrow to rest them.
Oxford's Dave Kemp.

That's one game over and 45 headaches to come.

Stoke manager Steve Cotterill after the opening day of the season.

We were woeful and I am embarrassed to be their manager.

Burnley boss Stan Ternent after a 3-0 defeat puts the Clarets bottom of Division One.

Last week's match was a real game of cat and dog.

Tranmere boss John Aldridge.

We attacked like Real Madrid but defended like a team from the Dog and Duck.

Huddersfield manager Mick Wadsworth after a 3-3 draw with Cheltenham Town.

Dave has this incredible knack of pulling a couple of chickens out of the hat each season. Mark McGhee

As a striker, you are either in a purple patch or struggling. At the moment, I'm somewhere in between. Bob Taylor

They're bound to finish bottom unless there's a place even lower in the bloody table. Peter Taylor on first surveying the scene at Hartlepool.

We're getting Port Vale into the First Division. One at a time! Stoke boss Ritchie Barker on signing three Port Vale players in as many months.

They're aren't many jock-straps to be found in our dressing-room, only nappies. Wrexham manager Brian Flynn on his emphasis on youth.

We are a young side that will only get younger. Paul Hart turns the clock back at Forest.

…after winning the Second Division championship we expected to settle down comfortably in our rightful place of mid-table mediocrity and expectations were low. Apart, of course, from the sort of people who queue up every week to wait for the turnstiles to open, dribble when they talk, and wear the entire contents of the club shop. Paul Gillman from Millwall's *The Lion Roars* fanzine.

There were no hiding places out there, and I had players putting their family jewels in front of the ball.
Manager Danny Wilson in praise of his Bristol City boys.

I don't know what it's like out there, but it's like an ice rink out there.
Stockport manager Andy Kilner.

For me to take the manager of the month award, I would have to win nine games out of eight. Sheffield United's Neil Warnock. *Observer* 2003

It would be foolish to believe that automatic promotion is automatic in any way whatsoever. Dave Bassett

They'll be dancing in the streets of Raith tonight. David Coleman fails to grasp that Raith Rovers play in Kircaldy.

The boys' feet have been up in the clouds since the win.
Alan Buckley

It looks as if I am trying to stab Dave Bassett in the back but I'm not holding a gun to anybody's head.
Micky Adams

We ended up playing football and that doesn't suit our style.
Frank admission from Airdrie manager Alex MacDonald.

Our performance today would not have been the best-looking bird but at least we got her in the taxi. She weren't the best-looking lady we ended up taking home but she was pleasant and very nice, so thanks very much and let's have a coffee.
QPR boss Ian Holloway on his side's 3-0 victory over Chesterfield. *The Guardian* 06/09/03

If the water stands still in the pond, it starts to stink.
QPR boss Ian Holloway goes all Cantona in explaining a desire for new signings.

I knew it wasn't going to be our day when I arrived at Links Park and found that we had a woman running the line. She should be at home making the tea or the dinner for her man who comes in after he has been to the football.

Albion Rovers manager Peter Hetherington, on the female official for his side's defeat to Montrose. *Independent* quotes of the year

The back four were like powder-puff girls, like the Tiller Girls. Rotherham's Ronnie Moore is unhappy with commitment levels at Millmoor.

Managing is a seven-day-a-week, almost 24-hour a day job. There's no rest and no escape, but I'm hooked on it. Barry Fry

It's a great job during the week, but sometimes the Saturday spoils it. Southport manager Mike Walsh.

It's a great job apart from Saturday afternoons.

Jocky Scott on the manager's job at Dunfermline.

It's a hard club to come to for players because from the moment you walk into the place you get the history rammed down your throat day in day out… you can't break wind without names like Clough and Birtles being mentioned. I know all the crap about winning the European Cup but the people who hang around the club pontificating haven't had the guts to become manager. Joe Kinnear ruffles feathers at Forest. *The Guardian* 16/02/04

We are the ailing patient. We moved to Milton Keynes to get over a serious illness, and now we are on a life-support with our organs removed, waiting for a miracle. Wimbledon manager Stuart Murdoch finds that the 2003/04 season is about to die on him. *Nuts*

I could do a better job than Vialli at Chelsea… sadly, people like me are not the in-thing right now. You need to be Italian, wear sunglasses, drive a beautiful car and know all about the beautiful game. The then Notts County boss Sam Allardyce shows he's not bitter.

Being manager of Barnet was like living with a double-decker bus on your head. When I left it was like it had been driven off. **Barry Fry lets his job get on top of him.**

A failed football club in October. A depressing place. Already, with seven months to go, the morning becomes a dread. **Eamon Dunphy describes Millwall in 1973.**

The place is like a morgue. Most of those that did come are moaning bastards. There's no home advantage for us. **Wimbledon manager Joe Kinnear bemoans another tiny attendance at Selhurst Park.**

Sunderland fans came to my door crying, something which had never happened before. Three generations of the one family came and left again, all of them crying. They just turned and went, never saw them before or since. **Niall Quinn recalls grief in Sunderland after a lost penalty shoot-out denied the Maccams a place in the Premiership.**

When I said even my Missus could save Derby from relegation, I was exaggerating.
Peter Taylor, ex-Cloughie sidekick.

I may be desperate but I'm not that desperate.
Middlesbrough's Dean Windass after refusing to join his father-in-law's team, North Ferriby United.

Although we are playing Russian roulette, we are obviously playing Catch 22 at the moment and that's a difficult scenario to get my head round. Paul Sturrock

I left as I arrived – fired with enthusiasm.
John McGrath on getting the bullet from Preston.

There were ten of us who used to hang around together in Streatham. At the last count, only two of us were on the outside [of prison]. Football was my way out and that was my fortune. Phil Babb reflects on his escape.

How could you finish your life as a sparky knowing that you could have been a professional footballer? What's security when you're 21, single, living with your parents and paying your mum £30 a week? Stuart Pearce on the moment he swapped an electrician's apprenticeship and a part-time contract at Wealdstone for Coventry City.

There are only two f*****g toilets, and they've run out of pies, coffee, f*****g everything. This is the worst ground I've ever been to in my f*****g life. Layer Road, Colchester, gets the thumbs-down from a Manchester City fan. *FourFourTwo:* 09/02

A 21st century stadium, with 14th century stewarding. An away fan's view of Home Park, Plymouth.

We were miles adrift at the bottom, our disciplinary record had seen us tot up more points than Johnny Logan in Eurovision, and through it all our tactics had become as predictable as Harry Potter at the box office. Y3KShakers.com, a Bury website.

Jesus turned water into wine. Kemp is turning Oxford into Accrington Stanley. Disgruntled Oxford fan Julia Toogood.

We didn't know James was going to get on. We heard a cheer just as we were getting in the car, turned on the radio and found out James had come on and scored. The family of Bournemouth striker James Hayter, who appeared as an 85th-minute substitute and scored a hat-trick. *The Guardian* 26/02/04

Coventry are the untouched bottle of Lea & Perrin's sauce at the back of the kitchen cupboard. Coventry are the pair of socks you meant to chuck out ages ago but have survived in the bottom drawer against all odds. Dave Cottrell in *90 Minutes* upsets the Highfield Road faithful.

I have been in some unbelievable scrapes, met some great characters, played at some mad clubs and I wouldn't swap any of it. It's just been a barrel of laughs right from the off. Steve Claridge on a career in the lower divisions.

I'll give you an Arsene Wenger answer – I didn't see the sending-off.
Acting Preston boss Kelham O'Hanlon takes a leaf from the master's book.

To be talking about vital games at this stage of the season is ridiculous, really, but tomorrow's game is absolutely vital. Brian Horton

If we stay there much longer, they might as well rename the league Rochdale Division Three.
Message on the club's official website.

People ask "What can John Fashanu bring to Northampton?" In a word, glamour. John Fashanu's method of becoming Mr Bojangles is to try and buy Northampton Town. *Observer* 25/01/04

I don't want him. I wouldn't mind if we gave him a Mickey Mouse role and he pumped a load of money in.
Bill Beattie, Sheffield Wednesday fan, on the possible appointment of Ken Bates.

When you've been thrown out of clubs like Barrow and Southport, you learn to live with disappointment.

Villa's Peter Withe on his omission from Bobby Robson's first England squad.

Come on Bury fans. You've got your night in the sun.

Adrian Chiles, Radio 5 Live.

I am manager of Macclesfield and am giving the job my total commitment. Obviously, as an Irishman, I want the job as their international manager.

Sammy McIlroy divides his loyalties.

There was Aldershot and training on dog-fouled public parks, where the central midfield player Giorgio Mazzon had a disabled sticker on his car... Journalist Ian Ridley describes life away from the limelight.

It's hard to shake off feeling like a bunch of peasants who found a diamond in the dirt, and then got shoved out the way as a bunch of rich kids pinched it.

Daniel Paul, Plymouth fan, on the loss of manager Paul Sturrock to Southampton.

George Best

Our talking point this morning is George Best, his liver transplant and the booze culture in football. Don't forget, the best caller wins a crate of John Smith's. **Alan Brazil, Talksport.**

The Dutch detailed Neeskens to mark George in that match. Neeskens was some player, but George made a monkey out of him and nut-megged the Dutch star so often that he finished by offering Neeskens a tie-up from his socks to tie his legs together. **Pat Jennings muses on George Best during a Northern Ireland game against Holland.**

When I'm on the field nothing gives me more pleasure than making a fool of somebody.

So that's what you look like, I've played you three times and all I've seen is your arse.

Welsh left-back Graham Williams to George Best after a 1963 international v Northern Ireland.

I'm better than Pele. I can kick with both feet.

I had nothing but contempt for the so-called hard men. For hard men I always read, men who couldn't play.

One day people might say I was another Ryan Giggs.

George Best turns the tables.

Forlan gets the ball inside the box, on the edge of the box and put it away from inside the box.

George forgets he's on air.

If the thinks he's got pressure now, things are going to get ten times worse. George Best on Wunderkind Wayne Rooney.

Independent quotes of the year

He wears a No. 10 jersey.
I thought it was his position but it turns out to be his IQ.

George Best on Paul Gascoigne.

Giggs came in from the left hand right.

Rumours that George was·drinking on duty failed to dispel.

Isn't he the one who can trap a ball as far as I can kick it?

George Best identifies Geoff Thomas.

I do not expect to play on a losing side. You'll find I have a nice personality when we start winning.

To call Keegan a superstar is stretching a point. Skill-wise, there a lot of better players around. He's not fit to lace my boots as a player.

George Best gets catty about Kev.

I was getting embarrassing. I didn't want to score any more, so I spent the last twenty minutes at left-back.

George Best gets bashful after scoring six in an FA Cup tie at Northampton.

The only thing that matters is football.

It wouldn't be possible for me to live like a monk to suit the demands of the game. I'd go mad. And now I burn the candle at both ends and drink too much, but I love the game and work hard at it.
George in 1970.

If I hadn't come back to football I'd be in the gutter right now. Either that or I'd have been sweeping the streets.
George predicts the future in thirty years, 1973.

People always say I shouldn't be burning my candle at both ends, maybe because they don't have a big enough candle.

They tell me to do so many things… shave off my beard, cut my hair, as if that would make me into what they wanted me to be. Jesus Christ had a beard and long hair and they didn't want to change him. George on being a style icon.

I couldn't get up and mingle even if I wanted to. There's always someone who wants to start a fight. Every time I go to the gents a couple of friends have to come along as well for protection.

When I get married everything will have to be perfect. The woman I marry will need to be a good cook.

It's always the same. When they're taking off their clothes they say they hope I don't think they're doing it just because I'm George Best.

I would like the girl I marry to be a virgin.

You can see sex in anything, depending on the way your mind works, but I don't suppose many girls get the chance to see a bloke running around with only a pair of shorts on very often. George loses his shirt.

I don't really class myself as a footballer.
I call myself an entertainer.

I'm not a caterer, I'm not really a businessman.
I'm a footballer. Everyone should try and do the
thing he does well; the thing I do well is football.

Skill is something I'll never lose.
I'll have that when I'm a hundred.

I was fascinated and felt rather
sorry for George Best when he
went through all his traumas.
Fame came to him when he
was so young. I've seen it
happen to so many young
people in the film business.
Elizabeth Taylor sympathises.

I feel awful for the person who died to save George. Alex Best, wife of George, responds to rumours that he was drinking again after a liver transplant. *Independent* quotes of the year

You may have heard this before, but I will respect this liver. After all, it's not mine. He didn't.

Once I started playing football, I realised I was in the perfect position for pulling birds. I had the limelight, the publicity, the money. Where could I go wrong?

I could never narrow my life down to the point where the only thing that mattered was the game. No-one knows how it feels to be me.

Was I the fifth Beatle? Not really.

The Price of Fame:

After this case, I don't think any club will allow a player to miss a drugs test again - and if a bus runs over me tomorrow and that's all we ever achieve then it was worth it for that. FA chief executive Mark Palios tempts fate after Rio Ferdinand is banned for eight months. *Independent* 03/01/04

In a restaurant one evening I saw middle-aged citizens rise suddenly and smash glasses and plates and hurl beefsteaks at each other in sheer frenzied delight when they heard over the radio that Uruguay had scored a point. US author John Gunther gets a culture shock.

The image of the British gentleman along the Belgian coast has given way to one of truculent and drunken youths, throwing cobblestones and wielding sticks. Belgian lawyer Jean-Marie Berkvens, after Manchester United 'fans' passed through Ostend.

The worst they can do is kill me. Controversial Turkish TV pundit Ahmet Cakar, shortly before being shot five times. *The Guardian* 28/02/04

Cruyff sometimes talks nonsense but it is always interesting nonsense.
Johann's biographer Nico Scheepmaker.

The day I start worrying about what the press think of me will be the day I pack it in. Tommy Docherty

Players have got a bigger responsibility than they realise. They have got to discipline themselves… they should only drink, gamble and womanise in moderation. Barry Fry

I was there the night Jock Stein died, and I want to go when I'm in bed with my beautiful young wife. Graeme Souness on stress.

I sent two players on to a fourth-storey roof to do some slating. We tried to get players down a pit but they wouldn't go because there was this small cavern they had to crawl through. When I was in Scotland I took my YTS people to a building site one day and slapped them in for an eight-hour shift. It made them appreciate they were in an easy life. Paul Sturrock keeps them on the straight and narrow. *The Guardian* 05/03/04

We've got a monster round our neck after beating England, but we must feed it. Socceroos' coach Frank Farina gets an appetite after Australia beat England.

We will win the European Cup. European football is full of cowards and we'll terrorise them. Malcolm Allison on the Manchester City side of the early '70s. They didn't.

We would like him to be our spiritual leader. Zong Bohong, Gansu team coach, on new signing Paul Gascoigne. *Independent* quotes of the year

Arsene Wenger has put me down a few times. The annoying thing is, he does it intelligently and I hate that. Sometimes I want to punch him on the nose. Tony Adams

I never miss Match of the Day. Cardinal Basil Hulme, 1978.

You lose too many times in this game not to celebrate when you win. Joe Mercer

The spirit he has shown has been second to none.
Terry Venables, commenting on Terry Fenwick's charge for drink-driving.

With the foreign players it's more difficult. Most of them don't even bother with the golf, they don't want to go racing. They don't even drink. Harry Redknapp

Very few of us have any idea of what life is like living in a goldfish bowl. Except of course, for those of us who are goldfish. Graham Taylor

He told you how to dress. He told you how to do your hair. Pre-war Arsenal and England international Eddie Hapgood on the influence of legendary manager Herbert Chapman.

Young players today unfortunately often prefer to act like stars in bars rather than on the playing field. Former French national manager Stevan Kovacs.

This game drives you either to drink or the madhouse… and I'm not going to the madhouse for anybody. Tommy Docherty

I like to go with him because he doesn't criticise. When I am home, whether we win or lose, he and I go the forest and I feel sometimes as if he will put his paw on my shoulder and say 'Don't worry, Helmut. Next time will be better.' Former West Germany manager Helmut Schoen takes comfort in his poodle.

The Football Association are looking for drugs in football. This sort of football is like a drug. It's like pot. You just want more and more of it. Bob Paisley reveals a surprising comparison.

If that guy was a woman I would be in danger of falling in love with him. Bill Shankly is impressed by Muhammad Ali.

If Luis Enrique was a girl, I'd marry him.

Former Spanish national coach Javier Clemente declares his affection.

My wife isn't talking to me. She blames me for what happened. My son Andy drove me home on Sunday night and isn't talking to me either. I'd left him out of the team and there was nothing he could do to save us. Bolton manager Colin Todd after the team's relegation from the Premiership.

I've been called a stupid Paddy over the years. You've just got to ignore it. David O'Leary

I can remember who was ready to whisper in an ear or two for their own ends. Now Vialli has found out that what goes round, comes round. Ruud Gullit on Vialli's sacking at Chelsea.

They [the fans] were waiting for us at the airport. I had police living in my home for 30 days. One or two of the other players were beaten up and had their cars smashed. Mexico captain Leonardo Cuellar recalls the price of failure after the 1978 World Cup.

You have to be diplomatic, but sometimes in training we kick each other because we don't like our team-mates. **Pavel Srnicek on dressing-room disharmony at Hillsborough.**

I want the West Ham fans to know that before I finish my career here we'll win something. Otherwise, I'll kill myself. **Paolo di Canio. (They didn't. Paolo moved to Charlton, still in rude health.)** *Observer* 2003

As far as I am concerned, with each day that I do not take a drink, I will always be a winner. **Tony Adams**

What's so great about reality? My reality stank. I was ready for a bender. **Tony Adams**

Did you know Alan Ball's missus used to come and watch us in training? One day she said to Keith Curle, 'You should have been tighter at the back.' Manchester City's Nicky Summerbee on having to endure advice from the manager's wife.

Without those cigarettes at half-time we could never have gone on. There would have been a mutiny. French international Georges Bayrou explains the need for relief during a 17-1 hammering from Denmark, 1908.

A few idiots have adorned my house in Middlesbrough with rotten eggs. There was also a murder threat in the mailbox. Christian Ziege recalls 'Boro fans unhappiness with his move to Spurs.

You're a disgrace to the family.

June Mullery, wife of Alan, in 1968. Mullery had become the first England player to be sent off.

It's not nice going into the supermarket when the woman at the checkout is thinking, 'dodgy keeper'. David James

They fiddled the draw so we wouldn't get to the Final on our own ground. Alex Ferguson cries foul after United were drawn against Real Madrid in the 2003 Champions League quarter-final.

I could not face the dinner. All I could think of was getting home as quickly as possible, shutting the doors, windows and curtains, and being left alone. Liverpool keeper Jerzy Dudek, after gifting Manchester United a win at Anfield.

If you missed a penalty you had your hair hacked off and were spat on by Uday's bodyguards. For every poor pass, you got a punch, and some players were forced to kick concrete balls in a prison yard. Habib Jaafer, Iraqi midfielder, recalls the horrors of 'coaching' from Saddam Hussein's son.

Our coach driver thinks he's Ben Hur, so I see prayer as an alternative to brakes. Congo national coach Mick Wadsworth on the reason for his leading prayer sessions at training. *The Guardian* 24/01/04

When you go to Derby four days after playing in Milan, you still have a picture of the San Siro in your head and it can be a shock. **Marcel Desailly on life at Stamford Bridge after Serie A.**

I know all about the Eric Cantonas of this world, with all their dosh. Great players but we're not all born like that. We've not all been so lucky. Some of us have had to work bloody hard to make it this far. **Vinnie Jones**

When the television people asked me if I'd like to play a football manager in a play, I asked how long it would take. They told me 'about ten days' and I said 'That's about par for the course'. **Tommy Docherty**

Sex could never be as great as winning the World Cup. It's not that sex isn't great, just that the World Cup is only once every four years. **Ronaldo**

Love is good for footballers, as long as it's not at half-time. **Danish coach Richard Moller Nielsen.**

Most Dangerous Opponent: My ex-wife.

Frank Worthington answers a questionnaire.

My son Mathieu called it a 'Ninja goal'. This is a result of me playing on his Playstation – it inspires me to try the craziest things. Laurent Robert on the inspiration behind his overhead kick special against Fulham *Nuts*

Who's the fat bloke in the number eight shirt?

Headline in *The Guardian*, following the discovery of football boots worn by Henry VIII. *The Guardian* 18/02/04

For a footballer, it's like living in a box. Someone takes you out of the box to train and play and makes all your decisions. I have seen players, famous internationals, in an airport lounge all get up and follow one bloke to the lav. Six of them, maybe, all standing there not wanting a piss, but following the bloke who does, like sheep.

Geoff Hurst

I suppose I'll have to get used to being called 'sir', but if a player gets formal on the field I will clobber him. Sir Alf Ramsey on his knighthood, 1967.

Some people think football is a matter of life and death. I don't like that attitude. I can assure them it is much more serious than that.

The oft-misquoted Bill Shankly.

I don't feel any different to when I was 25, maybe because I've always been this unfit. Graeme Le Saux

Must devote less time to sport if he wants to be a success.
Quote from Gary Lineker's school report.

Wayne mustn't allow himself to become crazy at his own success. He must just enjoy everything about his life and his football. Advice for Wayne Rooney from Ronaldo.

I wanted to be a garbage collector. He would drive pass my house with his horse and cart. I loved that. Hernan Crespo reveals modest childhood ambitions. *Independent* quotes of the year

It's about the drunken parties that go on for days – the orgies, the birds and the fabulous money.
Peter Storey, ex-Arsenal and England jailbird.

I'm finding it difficult to find a girlfriend in Barnsley or to settle into a decent way of life. The girls are far uglier than the ones back in Belgrade or Skopje and drink too much beer. **Georgi Hristov fails to make new friends.**

I've had a good rest, I've had holidays, got to know the wife again, but I've started itching recently. **A between-jobs Joe Royle.**

I am a Celtic man through and through and so I dislike Rangers because they are a force in Scottish football and therefore a threat to the club I love. **Maurice Johnston in 1988, one year before he joined Rangers.**

I don't think of foreigners as being professionals in the same sense as us. They're not prepared to give everything in the same way as our fellows. **Bobby Charlton in 1973, a long way from becoming an international ambassador.**

Malcolm McDonald uses the same conditioner as me. **Bob Ferris (Rodney Bewes) boasts to an unimpressed Terry Collier (James Bolam) in '70s sitcom Whatever Happened to the Likely Lads?**

Where's the dog track?

A star-struck Luther Blissett, on arriving at the San Siro from Vicarage Road.

When you look up into the crowd, what do you think about? Question at a press conference during a tour of China by Manchester United. *Observer* 2003

Once you've got a bull terrier, you never want another dog. I've got six bull terriers, a rottweiler and a bulldog. Julian Dicks

People will look at Bowyer and Woodgate and say 'Well, there's no mud without flames.' PFA chairman Gordon Taylor.

My own autobiography, which was written by Ian Ross...
Howard Kendall fails to bury his ghosts.

Jack cracks me up. He makes out he's not really interested in football and tells the whole world he's gone fishing. But we know what he's thinking about when he's fishing. Football. Johann Cruyff on Jack Charlton.

I was sorry to see O'Leary leave. So sad – in the appropriately mournful words of the late Ian Curtis, "How can something so good not function no more". He brought back life into the club, then threw it all away by publishing his memoirs. **Mark Monk of Leeds fanzine *Toellandback* sums up the O'Leary era.**

You can call me anything, but don't call me late for dinner. **William 'Fatty' Foulke, 24-stone goalkeeper for England, Chelsea, Sheffield United and Bradford.**

China feels great. I've tried chicken's head, chickens feet and bats and hopefully if I keep that up, I'll be flying. **Paul Gascoigne on life in the Far East.**

75% of what happens to Paul in his life is fiction. **Glenn Hoddle proves that it wasn't just Gazza who talked nonsense.**

He might be a great action man, but when it comes to football he hasn't got a bloody clue. **Kevin Beattie on Sylvester Stallone, during shooting of footie film Escape to Victory.**

It was partly the head of Maradona and partly the hand of God.
Diego's slant on that infamous goal.

If we see them on their coach on the way home we will give them a wave.

England's Teddy Sheringham after the defeat of Argentina at the 2002 World Cup.

I'm not really Jesus Christ. I'm lower down the line.
Ronaldo

There are only two Christs. One plays for Barcelona and the other is in heaven.

Hristo Stoichkov's homage to... himself.

I wasn't me making those saves, it was God.
Brazil's Taffarel owns up.

Was it a goal? Did the ball cross the line? Those two questions have haunted me most of my adult life. Geoff Hurst on 1966.

The new stadium helps, and it's something of which I am very proud. It was completed in 1998 to all UEFA and FIFA specifications and seats 3,548 people. Markus Schaper, general secretary of the Liechtenstein FA.

One Hump or Two? Title of Frank Worthington's autobiography.

When people ask me what was my biggest thrill in football, I can't help but think of Raquel Welch and the day she walked down the touchline at Stamford Bridge in a pair of skin-tight blue leather trousers. Much nicer than 'Chopper' Harris. Frank Worthington fails to keep his eye on the ball.

I would like to be a woman, though I don't know why. Auxerre striker Djibril Cisse gets in touch with his feminine side. *Independent* quotes of the year

I've never been to a club yet that hasn't had a few good fights, it's good for team spirit. Stuart Ripley on a man's game at Blackburn Rovers.

If you're so brave, go and enlist to fight in Iraq. Now get out of here. Terry Butcher confronts England's lunatic fringe at the Stadium of Light.

You should have seen them with their teeth out. What a sight. Spurs' Cyril Knowles after visiting the Liverpool dressing room.

When I see all my legs out, I have confidence. I look at my muscles and they look big and I feel strong. With big shorts, I can't see my muscles at all. Paolo di Canio on short shorts.

What time's the kick-off against Wolves? I can't afford to miss that one. Manchester United's Duncan Edwards, on a hospital bed after the Munich air crash. He died without leaving the hospital.

You should be dead.

Professor David Lloyd Griffiths, a surgeon, to Manchester City's Bert Trautmann after he had played on in the 1956 Cup Final, ignorant of his broken neck.

Coming to Manchester City, if anything, is more exciting than being at Real Madrid. Steve McManaman stretches credibility to breaking point. *Times*, 31/12/03

The last time this ground was seen on worldwide television, 'criminals' were being hung from the goalposts and shot in the centre circle.
Gary Mabbutt, member of the footballing taskforce in post-Taliban Afghanistan.

Although I've done that Pizza Hut advert, I've turned down lots of others offering to go down the missed-penalty route. Gareth Southgate

Since his arrival from West Ham, Michael Hughes' impact, like an elephant catapulted at an ant, has been considerable. Wimbledon's programme notes.

I like to be the tiger roaming the jungle or an eagle soaring over the skies. Sol Campbell on himself. *The Guardian* 06/09/03

I understand that Fashanu took his own masseur to the ground, and that is something that I can not condone. PFA secretary Gordon Taylor.

It's funny looking back, but I used to meet Vinnie Jones down the cafe; have sausage, egg, bacon, beans and a fried slice and then go off training. Now it's all pasta, rice and lots of vegetables. Dennis Wise on a balanced diet.

When Gordon came to Leeds, I was only 18 and he opened my eyes. He was supposed to be past it but I was amazed at how he lived his life. He even ate seaweed. Gary Speed on Gordon Strachan. *The Sun* 19/01/04

Not only did we introduce button-down collar shirts into the West Riding which, until then, were unheard of, we also started the Woolly Bully dance craze too. **Frank Worthington, bringing the Swinging Sixties to Yorkshire.**

One must keep to your line and style, be it fashionable or otherwise.
Germany's Rudi Voller gets sensitive about his mullet. *Observer* 2003

[While] I know it is irrational I have always been sensitive about my four sons' lack of hair… I have never been able to shake off the feeling that somehow the failure was mine; that I was responsible.
Cissie Charlton takes the rap for Bobby's combover.

I was the first man in Britain to own a tank top. **Frank Worthington on the pressures of being a style guru.**

For the players he left behind at Manchester United, there will be one lasting memory of Gary Birtles. His weird, way-out gear… the fancy bow ties, winged collars and spectacular suits that no-one else would wear without the courage of four bottles of wine.
Steve Coppell

I usually go out after a game wearing a normal suit; Versace, Armani, the same as what most of the lads wear. **David James**

I can't remember the last two Championships because I was drinking, so I'll savour every moment of this. Tony Adams on winning the Premiership with Arsenal in 1998.

I've attended a couple of funerals of lads who were lifelong Evertonians. At one, nobody was to wear black, just their Everton strip – even the Liverpudlians. Ex-Everton striker Graeme Sharp on unwavering loyalty.

Half at Highbury, half at White Hart Lane. Ian Wright's answer to the question: "Where would like your ashes scattered?".

I would say that more than 25% of football is gay. It's got to be higher than average. It's a very physical, closed world, a man's world, and you form deep bonds with people you hardly know. The late Justin Fashanu.

They do everything for you. We're treated like babies, really. So much so that there are some players, not necessarily at this club, who wouldn't know how to check in at an airport. Lee Dixon

Good strikers can only score goals when they have had good sex on the night before a match. **Romario reveals his pre-match training.**

More and more footballers' wives will cheat on their husbands because they are never at home. **Emmanuel Petit gets a suspicious mind.**

Who'd want a girl who plays football but can't make chapattis? **Jes is upbraided by her family during Brit-flick Bend it Like Beckham.**

If I hadn't been a footballer, I'd have been something else; for example, a priest. I mean, something different, something no-one else does. **Rodney Marsh**

Back then, you were made if your photo and an interview appeared in *Shoot*. Now all some players want is to get into *Hello* magazine. **Niall Quinn on youngsters today.**

When you get up at six o'clock in the morning to go to work and it's pitch black outside, and you know it will still be dark when you come home at night, that's when you appreciate being a professional footballer. **Ian Wright counts his blessings.**

We'll really shake 'em up, when we win the World Cup, 'cos Scotland is the greatest football team. From Ally's Tartan Army by Andy Cameron, 1978. We all know what happened next.

It is our opinion that the organisation we represent has not only let down one of our team-mates, but the whole of the England squad and its manager. We feel that they have failed us very badly. **Statement from the England squad after agreeing not to boycott a Euro 2004 qualifier in Turkey following Rio Ferdinand's removal.** *Times*, 31/12/03

They have hung him out to dry.
PFA's Gordon Taylor on the Ferdinand drugs-test controversy. *Times*, 31/12/03

I had eleven clubs, twelve if you count Stringfellows.

Frank Worthington on his less than homely lifestyle.

People think I had a square Afro, because it was so big it never fitted into photo frames and the papers and magazines had to crop it that way. George Berry, 1970s Wolves and Wales star. *Observer Sport Monthly*

He says his hair's natural. He must be using natural bleach.
Sunderland's Paul Bracewell on team-mate John Byrne.

I had shortish hair when I came here but I couldn't speak any English and so I couldn't go to the hairdresser to tell him what I wanted done. Juan Pablo Angel explains his long, lustrous locks. *Independent* 24/01/04

I am ugly, but what I do have is charm.
Self-portrait from Ronaldinho.

I was thrilled until I heard Ivan Lendl had finished above me.
Ally McCoist, after discovering he was named fifth best-looking sportsman in 1990.

When I presented my passport at Immigration they looked me up and down and said "No, no way." I asked what was wrong and they pointed at me, laughing "You? A footballer?" To them it meant big guys in helmets and shoulder pads. I had to explain I was a soccer player before they let me in. **Mickey Thomas encounters American indifference to the globe's biggest sport.**

It's like living in a cage.
Rosemary, wife of Pele, in 1970.

What I don't understand is how a Frenchman can be playing for Manchester United. He's not even from England.
Lord Denning QC overlooks E.C. employment law.

Why am I the best in the world? Because I am, that's all.
Chelsea's man of modesty, Claude Makelele. *Independent* quotes of the year

The game of football is like that. You win and you lose.
Pope Paul VI grasps the rudiments during an audience with Lazio in 1968.

My wife said she'd push me if I end up in a wheelchair.
Roy Keane

Their support can be an embarrassment at times, but I'd rather have them as an embarrassment than not at all. Then Manchester United manager Tommy Docherty on the club's notorious '70s following.

Nothing would stop me going to the Cup Final unless I was dead. And if I was dead, I'd want my ashes taken there.

MP and Chelsea fan Tony Banks before his team's Final appearance in 1997.

All of a sudden the place exploded and this rock came from the other side of the coach. It somehow missed four of the team playing dominoes, grazed Irving Nattrass on the arm, brushed past Frank's face and hit me on the forehead. Then it took a piece out of the card table where Malcolm MacDonald was sitting. My blood was all over the place. It ruined my suit, tie and trousers. Newcastle striker John Tudor remembers a missile being thrown through the window of the team bus, 1974.

I can't help wondering what I'm going to do when all this ends. Bobby Charlton in 1970.

I've been very lucky about injuries, actually. I've never had any trouble with my legs, or my knees… Gordon Banks in 1970. Two years later his career finished after he lost an eye in a car crash.

I don't have lucky signs except my teeth. Sometimes I play with them in and sometimes out. Martin Chivers

Fitness is confidence.
Stanley Matthews reveals the mystery ingredient.

A referee is facing divorce proceedings after he pulled a pair of knickers out of his pocket instead of a red card during a match. Carlos Jose Figueira Ferro… was so embarrassed that he ended the game with twenty minutes still to go, as his wife, watching, called lawyers… Report from *Terra*, Brazil. *Observer* 08/02/04

Professional footballers should have more sense than to consider marrying during the season. Anybody who does isn't behaving professionally as far as I'm concerned.

Bill Shankly

Ron Atkinson

Jari Litmanen should be made compulsory.

He's a little twat, that Totti. I can't see what all the fuss is about. Are there any sandwiches? I'm starving.

Big Ron offers piercing insight during the 2002 World Cup, unaware that the cameras are still rolling.

At least we were consistent – useless in defence, useless in midfield and crap up front.
Ron raves after Villa lose 3-0 at Coventry.

My goodness! You have been out of the Premiership a long time. Ron puts down an Ipswich steward who asked for identification.

It is the first time, after a match, that we've had to replace divots in the players. **Big Ron after Manchester United's encounter with a somewhat physical Valencia.**

I just bumped into Cyrille Regis and I said 'What's all this about you finding God? You worked with him at West Brom for four years'. **Ron on Cyrille Regis's born-again Christianity.**

That's not the type of header you want to see your defender make, with his hand.

Feyenoord don't have the answer to Pallister's mazy runs tonight, reminiscent of Gordon McQueen in his pomp.

That was Pele's strength, holding people off with his arm.

I always make sure I write Atkinson D on the teamsheet. Sometimes I wonder if I'm making a mistake. **Ron as Villa boss wonders whether selecting Dalian is a good idea.**

I never comment on referees and I'm not going to break the habit of a lifetime for that prat.

Our fans have been branded with the same brush.

Women should be in the kitchen, the discotheque and the boutique but not in football.

The ball goes down the keeper's throat where it hits him on the knees to say the least.

How can anybody call this work? People in this game don't realise how lucky they are. You drive to the ground, play a few five-a-sides, then have lunch. Big Ron on his managerial lot at Aston Villa.

He'll take some pleasure from that, Brian Carey. He and Steve Bull have been having it off all night.

He's the worst finisher since Devon Loch. When he's in a clear shooting position he's under orders to do just one thing… pass. **Ron on Carlton Palmer.**

If that was a penalty, I'll plait sawdust.

I've just seen Gary Lineker shake hands with Jurgen Klinsmann – it's a wonder Klinsmann hasn't fallen over.

Now Manchester United are 2-1 down on aggregate, they are in a better position than when they started the game at 1-1.

You can see the ball go past them, or the man, but you'll never see both man and ball go past at the same time. So if the ball goes past, the man won't, or if the man goes past they'll take the ball.

They've picked their heads up off the ground, and now they have a lot to carry on their shoulders.

We haven't had a strategic free kick all night. No one's knocked over attackers ad lib.

You know when I say that things happen in matches. Well, it just happened there.

If that's Junior Baiano, I wouldn't like to meet Senior Baiano.

He's what is known in some schools as a f**king lazy thick n****r.

Ron's thoughtless and offensive parting shot aimed at Chelsea's Marcel Desailly.

Own Goal

For the first time I'm at a club where I believe I've got a chance to win it.
Terry Venables on his appointment as manager of Leeds. They finished 15th; Venables failed to finish the season.

Without naming names, the PFA have got to get involved and start naming and shaming divers. Joe Royle

Football, it's an old, funny game.
Gianluca Vialli nearly gets his order in the right words.

Brazil – they're so good it's like they are running around the pitch playing with themselves.
John Motson

The underdogs will start favourites for this match.
Craig Brown

Ireland is not a bar of chocolates.
Georgian international Alexander Rekhviashvili sets his sights on the Premier League rather than the Emerald Isle.

One year I played fifteen months.
Franz Beckenbauer turns the clock forward.

The Saudis would struggle in Europe because of that problem with those prayers five times a day. You don't know if they're going to turn up for training. I'm being serious. Don Howe joins the diplomatic corps.

In-match dactyl sodomisation.
Spanish FA's official take on the antics of Sevilla's Pablo Alfaro, who was caught on camera inserting his finger into an opponent's rectum. *Observer* 08/02/04

I will die a Catholic, I will die an Arsenal fan and I will die a Tory.
Former Conservative MP Chris Patten.

I have seen Manchester United so many times on the television this season and they were playing really poor football, really rubbish. There is no doubt we are the best football team in England.
Patrick Viera after United have beaten Arsenal to the title, May 2003. *Observer* 28/12/03

Nah, Pele's the black Rodney Marsh.

Marsh responds to being referred to as 'the white Pele'.

I don't really like the North. It's always raining, it's very cold and I don't like all those little houses. Frederic Kanoute ensures a warm reception on away grounds north of Watford.

I am so sorry. I have been unable to sleep after what happened... I promise I will replace this unhappy situation with happy things. Jose Antonio Reyes, after his first goal for Arsenal is past his own keeper. *Independent* 07/02/04

...when Flitcroft played for the A team, he had 'footballer' written all over his forehead. Colin Bell

I spent four indifferent years at Everton, but they were good years. Martin Hodge

For those of you watching in black and white, Spurs are in the yellow strip. **John Motson**

I'm not convinced that Scotland will play a typically English game. **Gareth Southgate**

If there wasn't such a thing as football, we'd all be frustrated footballers. **Mike Lyons**

All the Leeds team are 100% behind the manager, but I can't speak for the rest of the squad. **Brian Greenhoff**

I still don't know if the shot was in or not. I have to say that I was standing in a poor position for that shot, exactly head-on instead of diagonal with the goal. I wouldn't have allowed the goal if Bakhramov hadn't pointed to the middle with his flag. **Gottfried Dienst, 1966 World Cup Final referee, on that goal...**

I was inbred into the game by my father.
David Pleat keeps it in the family.

I'd give my right arm to get back into the England team. Peter Shilton cuts off his nose...

It wasn't a bad performance but you can't tell whether it was good or bad. Jimmy Hill

Terry Venables has literally had his legs cut off from underneath him three times while he's been manager.
Barry Venison

Hierro has been magnificent for the Spaniards tonight.
TV pundit Dion Dublin gives his verdict. One problem; Hierro wasn't playing.

We are now in the middle of the centre of the first half. David Pleat

It's the end-of-season curtain raiser. Peter Withe

We're not used to weather in June in this country.
Jimmy Hill

If you just came into the room and didn't know who was who, you'd obviously say Newcastle looked the most likely to score. Terry Paine

It's a football stadium in the truest sense of the word.
John Motson

He's got a brain under his hair.
David Pleat

If history is going to repeat itself I think we can expect the same thing again. **Terry Venables**

I can't fault Mark Palios too highly. **John Motson**

They've missed so many chances they must be wringing their heads in shame. **Ron Greenwood**

Merseyside derbies usually last 90 minutes and I'm sure this one won't be any different. **Trevor Brooking**

It's one of the greatest goals ever, but I'm surprised people are talking about it as the goal of the season. **Andy Gray**

I think that their young legs would have found younger hearts inside them. Jimmy Armfield seldom wears his heart on his sleeve.

It may have been going wide, but nevertheless it was a great shot on target. Terry Venables

Zola's got two feet. David Pleat wins Big Ron's spotter's badge...

He held his head in his hands as it flashed past the post. Alan Brazil

The goals made such a difference to the way this game went. John Motson

Venison and Butcher are as brave as two peas in a pod. John Sillett

He was as game as a pebble.
David Webb's commentating career sinks like a stone.

Once Tony Daley opens his legs, you've got a problem. Howard Wilkinson

Most of the players will be wearing rubbers tonight.
Gary Lineker

They've come out with all cylinders flying.
Luther Blissett

Apart from their goals, Norway wouldn't have scored. Terry Venables

It was a definite penalty but Wright made
a right swansong of it. Jack Charlton

I'd be surprised if all 22 players are on
the field at the end of the game – one's
already been sent off. George Best

The World Cup is a truly international event.
John Motson

The World Cup is every four
years, so it's going to be a
perennial problem. Gary Lineker

If England are going to win this match, they're
going to have to score a goal. Jimmy Hill

Seaman, just like a falling oak, manages to change direction.
John Motson

Well, I've seen some tackles Jonathan, but that was the ultimatum. Alan Mullery

For such a small man Maradona gets great elevation on his balls.
David Pleat

We were a little bit outnumbered there, it was two against two. Frank McLintock

That's a 1,415-pointer there if there ever was one.
Barry Venison fails his six times table.

The tackles are coming in thick and thin. Alan Brazil

The candle is still very much in the melting pot. Alan McInally

Hearts are now playing with a five-man back four.
Alan McInally

All the cul-de-sacs are closed for Scotland.
Joe Jordan

The Scots have really got their hands cut out tonight. Trevor Francis

The club has literally exploded.
Ian Wright

He's like all great players but he's not a great player yet. Trevor Francis

Historically, the host nations do well in Euro 2000. Trevor Brooking

That would have been the icing on his start.
David Pleat

Barnsley have started off the way they mean to begin. Chris Kamara

The game is balanced in Arsenal's favour.
John Motson

If plan A fails, he could always revert to plan A. Mark Lawrenson

If there's one thing Gus Uhlenbeek's got, it's pace and determination. Ray Houghton

It's his first cap, so he's not got a lot of experience at this level.
Brian Marwood

…and for those of you watching without television sets, live commentary is on Radio 2. David Coleman

If they play together, you've got two of them.
Dion Dublin

The 3-5-3 system isn't working for them.
Eamonn Dunphy goes up to eleven.

He didn't get booked for the yellow card.
Frank Stapleton

He hasn't been the normal Paul Scholes today, and he's not the only one. Alvin Martin

Scotland don't have to score tonight, but they do have to win. **Billy McNeill**

It's real end-to-end stuff, but unfortunately it's all up at Forest's end. Chris Kamara

…the Derby fans walking home absolutely silent in their cars. **Alan Brazil**

He hits it into the corner of the net as straight as a nut.
David Pleat

He has all-round, 365-degree vision.
Alan Mullery

There's Thierry Henry, exploding like the French train that he is. David Pleat

It seems that they're playing with one leg tied together. Kenny Sansom

...so different from the scenes in 1872, at the Cup Final none of us can remember. John Motson

Gerry Taggart has been booked for a caution. Dave Bassett

I don't think anyone enjoyed it. Apart from the people who watched it. Alan Hansen

This is a real cat and carrot situation. David Pleat

It's imperable that they get off to a good start. Charlie Nicholas

It's like the Sea of Galilee, the two defenders just parted. Mark Lawrenson

Even if he had scored for Alaves, it would have made no difference to the scoreline. Gerry Armstrong

Michael Owen isn't the tallest of lads, but his height more than makes up for that. Mark Lawrenson

When it comes to the David Beckhams of this world, this guy's up there with Roberto Carlos. Duncan McKenzie

They're in pole position *ie* 3rd position for the Champions' League. Mark Lawrenson

He's got a great future ahead. He's missed so much of it.
Terry Venables

These managers all know their onions and cut their cloth accordingly. Mark Lawrenson

The midfield picks itself; Beckham, Scholes, Gerrard and A.N. Other. Phil Neal

Paolo Wanchope has scored on 67 minutes and that's exactly the start Manchester City would have wanted. Dave Bassett

And Arsenal now have plenty of time to dictate the last few seconds. Dave Bassett

If the goalkeeper wasn't there, it would have been a goal. Dave Bassett

And what a time to score! 22 minutes gone. John Motson

Well Terry, can you tell us where you are in the League, how far you are ahead of the second team? Ian St John

Not only has he shown Junior Lewis the red card, but he's sent them off. Chris Kamara

I think you and the referee were in a minority of one, Billy. Jimmy Armfield

Let's close our eyes and see what happens.
Jimmy Greaves

It was a fair decision, the penalty, even though it's debatable whether it was inside or outside the box.
Bobby Charlton

Paul Gascoigne has recently become a father and been booked for over celebrating. John Motson

He's perfectly fit, apart from his physical fitness. Mike England

It is a cup final and the one who wins it goes through. Jimmy Hill

The only thing Norwich didn't get was the goal they finally got. Jimmy Greaves

They can crumble as easily as ice cream in this heat. Sammy Nelson

We sometimes think of Arsene Wenger as a general media population. Rodney Marsh

There's going to be four of five teams battling for the top six spots. Chris Waddle

The time in the world has gotten shorter so it doesn't take so long to get to Australia. Phil Neal bids to be the new Dr. Who.

There are so many teams now down at the bottom of the Third Division. The FA really has to do something about it. **Peter Lorimer**

This game could go either way. Or it could be a draw. Peter Lorimer stays on the fence.

I was here at Maine Road when City lost 4-0 to Wimbledon, but they could have been 2-0 up after five minutes, and if they had been, the final score might just have been different. **Jim Beglin**

Roy Evans bleeds red blood.
Alan Mullery

It's a tense time for managers. They have to exhume confidence. **Gary Lineker**

We got the winner with three minutes left but then they equalised. Ian McNail

He looks as if he's been playing for England all his international career. Trevor Brooking

It was one of those shots that flew straight along the floor. Jimmy Armfield

Michael Owen is not a diver. He knows when to dive, and when not to. Steve Hodge

Roy Keane didn't go through the book with a fine toothbrush. Tony Cascarino

The first two-syllable word I learned when I was growing up was 'discretion'. Eamonn Dunphy

1-1 is probably a fair reflection of the score at half-time. Frank Stapleton

It's so vital if you can win the game one-nil rather than lose it one-nil. Billy Bonds

You have to remember that some of these guys are playing in front of the live cameras.
Tony Gale

You're not sure if the ball is going to bounce up or down.
Frank Stapleton

There is still nothing on the proverbial scoreboard.
John Motson

PSV have got a lot of pace up front. They're capable of exposing themselves. Barry Venison

They've got one man to thank for that goal, Alan Shearer. And they've also got to thank referee Chris Wilkie.
Chris Kamara

Solskjaer never misses the target. That time he hit the post.
Peter Schmeichel

Djimi Traore had to adapt to the English game and he did that by going out on loan to Lens last season. Ian Rush

The Swedish back four is amongst the tallest in the World Cup. Their average height is 7 foot 4. Chris Waddle

He talks not probably enough yet, due to the experience he hasn't got. Chris Waddle

He was in a no-win situation, unless he won the match.
Murdo MacLeod

Eighty per cent of teams who score first in matches go on to win them. But they may draw some. Or occasionally.
David Pleat

It's what I call one of those 'indefensible' ones, you can't defend against them. Andy Gray

He's hardly been on the pitch as many times as he's played.
Alvin Martin

Peter Beardsley has got a few tricks up his book.
Ian Snodin

The fact that Burnley got beat here already will stick in their claw. Mark Lawrenson

Nearly all the Brazilian supporters are wearing yellow shirts. It's a fabulous kaleidoscope of colour.
John Motson

Every time they attacked, we were memorised by them.
Charlie Nicholas

He signals to the bench with his groin. **Mark Bright**

It's slightly alarming the way Manchester United decapitated against Stuttgart. **Mark Lawrenson**

Bruce has got the taste of Wembley in his nostrils. **John Motson**

Manchester United have hit the ground running, albeit with a three-nil defeat.
Bob Wilson

They get to about 30 yards out and then everything goes square and a bit pedantic. Charlie Nicholas

Bridge has done nothing wrong, but his movement's not great and his distribution's been poor. Alan Mullery

He's not the sharpest sandwich in the picnic.
Tony Cascarino *Private Eye* 20/02/04

I expect Chelsea to make a record signing in the near distant future. Tony Cascarino

Had we not got that second goal the score might well have been different. David Pleat *Private Eye* 20/02/04

It looks like a one-man show here although there are two men involved.
John Motson

It's hard to imagine Crouch scoring his second had he not scored his first. Hyder Jawad, Birmingham Post. *Private Eye* 20/02/04

Tempo. Now, there's a big word.
Barry Venison

He's had two cruciates and a broken ankle. It's not easy that. Every player attached to the club is praying the boy gets a break. Alex Ferguson on Wes Brown. *Observer* 04/01/04

It is important to win the games, particularly when the fish are down. Gianluca Vialli cashes in his chips.

That's an old Ipswich move – O'Callaghan crossing for Mariner to drive over the bar.
John Motson

Coventry, in all honesty, never really looked like scoring. Alex Ferguson misses the finer points of a 3-2 defeat at Highfield Road.

We had a pedantic tempo in the first half. We tittered on the edge of nervous stability. Sam Allardyce laughs off a Bolton performance, sort of. *The Guardian* 19/01/04

No-one hands you cups on a plate.
Terry McDermott

If you can get through the first round, you have a good chance of getting into the next one. Nigel Worthington

Not quite the first half you might have expected, even though the score might suggest that it was. John Motson

Tore's got a groin strain and he's playing with it. Alex McLeish predicts premature short-sightedness for Tore Andre Flo.

He lacks that confidence which he possesses. Martin O'Neill

A bit of retaliation there, though not actually on the same player. Frank Stapleton

Of their goals, two came from headers and one was a header.
Joe Royle

We signed to play until the day
we died, and we did. Jimmy Greaves

As with every young player, he's only eighteen.
Alex Ferguson

In football, you can never say anything is
certain. The benchmark is 38-40 points.
That has always been the case. That will
never change. Steve Bruce

Matches don't come any bigger than
FA Cup quarter-finals. Neil Warnock

It was a continuance of what we have seen this season. That is, various clubs beating each other.
Ron Noades

And I suppose they [Spurs] are nearer to being out of the FA Cup now than any other time since the first half of this season, when they weren't ever in it anyway. John Motson

The gelling period has just started to knit.
Ray Wilkins knits jelly

It's Arsenal 0 Everton 1, and the longer it stays like that the more you've got to fancy Everton to win. John Motson

Statistics are there to be broken.
Chris Kamara

Leeds have only had one shot on target, which may well have been the goal. Andy Gray

As long as you have a hole in your arse, you'll never make a footballer. Fulham manager Malcolm Macdonald to teenage triallist Niall Quinn.

Their keeper played very well and it was not the best pitch but I am not making excuses. Graham Rix

The unexpected is always likely to happen. John Motson

Whoever wins the Championship today will win the Championship no matter who wins. Denis Law

Unfortunately, we don't get a second chance. We've already played them twice. Trevor Brooking

The match has become quite unpredictable, but it still looks as though Arsenal will win the Cup. John Motson

The beauty of cup football is that Jack always has a chance of beating Goliath. Terry Butcher

Chelsea haven't got any out-and-out strikers on the bench unless you count Zenden, who's more of a winger. John Motson

It was the first four goals that cost us the game. Southampton manager David Jones picks up a bleedin' obvious award.

The Arsenal defence is
skating close to the wind.
Jack Charlton

Whether that was a penalty or not,
the referee thought otherwise. **John Motson**

We looked all around Europe
for people with any credentials,
but it is a fact that anyone who
is any good was already tied
up with a job. **Alan Sugar unveils Christian Gross as**
manager of Tottenham.

The referee is wearing the same yellow-coloured top as the Slovakian goalkeeper. I'd have thought the UEFA official would have spotted that, but perhaps he's been deafened by the noise of this crowd. John Motson

The Blackburn crowd have been saturated by fifty thousand Newcastle fans. Brian Little

I've been asked that question for six months. It's not fair to expect me to make such a fast decision on something that has been put upon me like that. Terry Venables

I was a young lad when I was growing up.
David O'Leary

I watched the game, and I saw an awful lot of it. Andy Gray

I saw him kick the bucket over there, which suggests he's not going to be able to continue. Trevor Brooking

I know that Gareth Barry has been told by Howard Wilkinson to take a long hard look at these with his left foot. John Motson

I don't want to be either partial or impartial.
Frank McLintock

Kevin Keegan said that if he had a blank sheet of paper, five names would be on it. Alvin Martin

Kevin Keegan

I came to Nantes two years ago and it's much the same today, except that it's totally different.

You get bunches of players like you do bananas, though that is a bad comparison.

I'll never play at Wembley again, unless I play at Wembley again.

In the dressing room at the interval, I told the lads that we'd be playing for pride and that I'd be praying for a miracle. Keegan's team-talk to Manchester City, 3-0 down to Spurs with ten men at White Hart Lane. They won 4-3. *The Evening Standard*, 05/02/04

Keegan couldn't have made a bigger impact had he descended into the Kippax hospitality suite on a cloud flanked by horn-blowing Raphaelesque angels and wearing a crown. His arrival at Maine Road was triumphant, only nymphs throwing rose petals into his path were missing. *Bert Trautman's Helmet,* Manchester City fanzine, on Keegan's managerial entrance.

Part of me will always be in Newcastle. My house is still there…

It's like a toaster, the ref's shirt pocket. Every time there's a tackle, up pops a yellow card.

Shaun Wright-Phillips has got a big heart. It's as big as him, which isn't very big, but it's bigger.

I don't think there's anyone bigger or smaller than Maradona.

Chile have three options, they could win or they could lose.

There'll be no siestas in Madrid tonight.

The good news for Nigeria is that they're two-nil down very early in the game.

Argentina won't be at Euro 2000 because they're from South America.

The Germans have only one player under 22, and he's 23.

He can't speak Turkey, but you can tell he's delighted.

England have the best fans in the world and Scotland's fans are second to none.

There's a slight doubt about only one player and that's Tony Adams, who definitely won't be playing tomorrow.

In some ways, cramp is worse than having a broken leg.

The substitute is about to come on. He's a player who was left out of the starting line-up today.

You need 88 points for the title and we've got 61 at present with sixteen games to go, but if you set targets you limit yourself.

You can't do better than go away from home and get a draw.

Nicolas Anelka left Arsenal for £23m and they built a training ground on him.

I know what is round the corner, I just don't know where the corner is. But the onus is on us to perform and we must control the bandwagon.

Jaap Stam is like Steve Bould on roller-skates...
he's as strong as a tree-trunk, but more mobile.
David Pleat can't see the wood for the trees.

He chanced his arm with his left foot. Trevor Brooking

England now have three fresh men with three fresh legs. Jimmy Hill

At first he told us to wear boxing gloves in bed on Friday nights, then later he would tell us to send the wife to her mother. Ian St John remembers Bill Shankly's tips for avoiding pre-match relations.

All referees are incompetent. I can't think of a single one doing a decent job.

Ian Wright

Suzuki's got a good engine.
Mark Lawrenson on Japanese striker Suzuki Takayuki.

Wimbledon are putting balls into the blender.
Rodney Marsh

They didn't change positions, they just moved the players around.
Terry Venables reveals why his coaching ability is so highly regarded.

Zoff's alright on the high stuff but on low shots he's been going down in installments.
Ian St. John is critical of Italy's World Cup winning captain.

It's end to end stuff, but from side to side.
Trevor Brooking

Wanchope... His full name, Paolo Cesar Wanchope Watson. Why didn't he decide to be called Watson? Barry Davies

I feel that it's like a bomb, a time bomb that can explode, the good or the bad way. Former Chelsea boss Ruud Gullit on the Abramovich era at Stamford Bridge. *Observer Sport Monthly,* 08/02/04

Back then unless you took a machete out on the pitch you wouldn't get booked.

Jimmy Greaves reflects on a less beautiful game.

Whelan was in the position he was, exactly.

Incisive stuff from Jimmy Armfield.

If football were meant to be Art, God wouldn't have invented Carlton Palmer.

Dominik Diamond offers a moment of wisdom.

The game you are about to see is the most stupid, appaling, disgusting and disgraceful exhibition of football, possibly in the history of the game.

David Coleman introduces highlights of the 'Battle of Santiago', Chile v Italy, in 1962.
Observer Sport Monthly

Di Matteo's taken to playing in midfield like a duck out of water.

Peter Osgood

The game is about glory. It's about doing things in style, with a flourish, about going out and beating the other lot, not waiting for them to die of boredom. Danny Blanchflower votes for style over sterility.

Football's football. If that weren't the case it wouldn't be the game it is. Garth Crooks

In the words of the old song, 'it's a long time from May to December' but, you know, it's an equally long time from December to May.
Jimmy Hill

Mick McCarthy will have to replace Cascarino because he's quickly running out of legs.
Mark Lawrenson

Those are the sort of doors that get opened if you don't close them.
Terry Venables

A round ball and a square goal suggest the shape of the Yin and the Yang.
Li Yu (50-130 AD), Chinese writer, describes a prototype of the beautiful game.

He's good at that, David Beckham. He's good at kicking the ball.
Trevor Booking blinds us with science.

It really is an amazing result, nil-nil at half time.
Chris Kamara

Cheating and diving is no sin if you win.
Paolo Montero of Juventus fails the audition for Corinthian Casuals. *Observer* 2003

If a week is a long time in politics, then for Ron Atkinson's Manchester United, the last seven days have been an equinox. Stuart Hall

Hodge scored for Forest after 22 seconds, completely against the run of play. Peter Lorenzo, BBC Radio 2.

Borussia Moenchengladbach 5 Borussia Dortmund 1. So, Moenchengladbach win the Borussia derby.
Gary Newbon

Clearly, Graeme, it all went according to plan. What was the plan exactly?
Souness's tactics prove too cunning for Elton Welsby.

Football games turn on things that are done by players. Willie Miller

I think that France, Germany, Spain, Holland and England will join Brazil in the semi-finals. Pele fails to do his sums.

Achtung! Surrender

Mindless Mirror headline before the England v Germany semi-final in Euro 96.

Two soccer points to no score.

A US website reports the nation's 2-0 victory over Mexico at the 2002 World Cup.

The Belgians will play like their fellow Scandinavians, Denmark and Sweden. Andy Townsend

Germany are probably, arguably, undisputed champions of Europe.

Bryan Hamilton

The maestro appears to be dribbling towards Millet's but could easily swerve across the street to Woolworth's.

Graham Hart, editor of the Guinness *Football Encyclopedia,* on the statue dedicated to Stanley Matthews in Stoke.

Chris Waddle is off the pitch at the moment, exactly the position he is at his most menacing.

Gerald Sinstadt

Chelsea last won away on April Fool's Day. Now it's Boxing Day, another great religious holiday.

Dominic Johnson

To be fair, I don't think Les Ferdinand was fouled there. I think he went over on his own ability.

Alan Mullery

John Bond has bought a young left-sided midfield player who, I guess, will play on the left side of midfield. **Jimmy Armfield**

George will be happy with a draw. I know how ambitious and positive he is. **Terry Neill**

Romania are more Portuguese than German.
Barry Venison

The Newcastle back three, back four, back five have been at sixes and sevens.
Barry Venison

If Jennings had been available on that memorable occasion when the Roman met the Etruscans, Horatius surely would have had to be satisfied with a seat on the substitutes bench. *The Guardian* gets carried away after Pat Jennings has a decent game at Leeds.

'...famous for missing open goals and for the inexorable precision with which he would find the goalpost'.

Italian newspaper's verdict on Luther Blissett's lone season for Milan. *Observer Sport Monthly*

He [Shearer] wouldn't have scored 30-odd a season in the '70s. He'd have had players like me and Tommy Smith kicking great big f*****g lumps out of him and he wouldn't have got a look in. Ron Harris

Every British male, at some time or other, goes to his last football match. It may well be his first football match.

Martin Amis fails to appreciate the beautiful game.

Batistuta gets most of his goals with the ball.
Ian St John

Ronaldo is always very close to being onside or offside. Ray Wilkins

Swan Lake on turf.

Kenneth Wolstenholme's description of the 1960 European Cup Final at Hampden Park; Real Madrid 7 Eintracht Frankfurt 3.

To say that these men paid their shillings to watch twenty-two hirelings kick a ball is merely to say that a violin is wood and catgut, that Hamlet is so much paper and ink. For a shilling the Bruddersford United AFC offered you conflict and art...' JB Priestley in *The Good Companions*, 1929.

England have been beaten by the Mickey Mouse and Donald Duck team.

US press comment after the Americans humbled England 1-0 at the 1950 World Cup.

Wembley is just one huge satsuma at the moment.

John Inverdale talks fruity nonsense.

The new West stand casts a giant shadow over the pitch, even on a sunny day.

Chris Jones in the *Evening Standard*.

The Brazilians aren't as good as they used to be, or as they are now.
Kenny Dalglish

Our football comes from the heart, theirs from the mind.
Pele, when asked the difference between football in South America and Europe.

That's bread and butter straight down the goalkeeper's throat. Andy Gray

I might have said that, but on the whole I talk a lot of rubbish.
A frank Eric Cantona denies rumours he might return to football as a coach.
Times, 31/12/03

Long Live the Mother who Gave Birth to You
Headline in Spanish sports' daily *Marca* after Spain's 4-3 defeat of Yugoslavia at Euro 2000.

It's only twelve inches high. It is solid gold. And it undeniably means England are the champions of the world.Kenneth Wolstenholme

John Harkes going to Sheffield, Wednesday.
Headline from the *New York Post*, 1993.

United are hated, are they? I haven't noticed that. I must be out of touch. **Denis Law catches up with the rest of the country.**

Soon there were bodies everywhere, blue with death... I had come to photograph Platini and had ended up photographing war. **Photographer Eamonn McCabe reveals the horror of the Heysel disaster.**

He carried on alone, blew out his cheeks, and beat Tilkowski with a terrible left footer. **Brian Glanville describes Geoff Hurst's goal in the 1966 World Cup Final.**

I'm going to sue Alan Hansen as he used to make me head all the balls. If I get Alzheimer's in ten years, I'm going to take civil action against him. **Mark Lawrenson on former centre-back partner Alan Hansen.**

He's got a knock on his shin there, just above the knee. **Frank Stapleton**

The lad got over-excited when he saw the whites of the goalposts' eyes. Steve Coppell

He's probably already forgotten about that bang on the neck.
BBC commentator Kenneth Wolstenholme, on Manchester City 'keeper Bert Trautmann after the 1956 Cup Final. Trautmann's neck was later found to be broken.

Korsten is making a meal of it... er... that's clearly a penalty.

Trevor Francis hedges his bets.

Okon was booked for tackling Hamman's tackle.
Dave Bassett

This fellow Tardelli, he's likely to leap out of the TV at us. He's put more scar tissue on people than the surgeons at Harefield hospital. Jimmy Greaves gets scared.

I received the ten shillings in expenses, returned to my cosy middle-class house and turned my back on pro-football to embark on a proper job. Stuart Hall on the moment he swapped the playing field for the microphone.

Wife-beating is a despicable activity. But I do not see how Glenn Hoddle could have excluded Paul Gascoigne from the England team on this. Hoddle is a manager not a judge of morals. Johnny Giles in the *Daily Express*.

If every manager in Britain were given his choice of any one player to add to his team some, no doubt, would toy with the idea of Best; but the realists, to a man, would have Bremner. John Arlott in *The Guardian* on Billy Bremner.

Football, wherein is nothing but beastly fury and extreme violence, whereof proceedeth hurt, and consequently rancour and malice do remain with them that be wounded. Thomas Elyot, *Book of the Governor,* 1531 (Vinnie Jones wasn't even born for another 434 years).

It's just a round thing you kick to another player, hmmm? Isn't it? Wasn't it? Er... Ron Manager

Hagi has got a left foot like Brian Lara's bat.
Don Howe

German players have turned the dive into an art form.
FIFA president Sepp Blatter.

The game should be a two-act play with 22 players on stage and the referee as director.
Referee Ken Aston gets theatrical.

He was the first great superstar. With only newspapers and radio and TV just starting, everybody knew Stanley Matthews. Jimmy Armfield

I've never even heard of Senegal.
From Paul Gascoigne's mercifully brief spell as an ITV panelist during the 2002 World Cup finals.

The difference between right and wrong is often not more than five metres.
Johann Cruyff

We love Brazil because they are Braziiiiiiiiil.

Alex Bellos puts the samba into that second syllable.

Argentinian police are hunting for Diego Maradona's missing penis.

The plastic device – used by the player to cheat drugs tests in the 90s – disappeared while on loan from a Buenos Aires museum. *The Star* report the ultimate piss-take.
Observer 04/01/04

At half-time the game's virginity was still intact.
Clement Freud

A woman on her wedding day – nervous, out of position and hoping everything would soon be over so she could go up to the bedroom. Spanish newspaper *Marca* gives its verdict on Fabien Barthez' performance for Manchester United against Real Madrid.

Football is a game you play with the ball, not the legs.

David Ginola explains his work-rate.

The fans like to see Balde wear his shirt on his sleeve. Kenny Dalglish

A game is not won until it's lost.
David Pleat

Which planet are you from? I am going to cry! Oh, my God! How beautiful soccer is! What a goal! Diego Maradona! You make it seem so easy! I am crying, forgive me please!
Argentine commentator Victor Hugo Morales celebrates the second against England at the 1986 World Cup. *Observer Sport Monthly*

I think that's lack of width with his height.
Trevor Brooking

We've sold our birthright down the fjord to a nation of seven million skiers and hammer throwers who spend half their lives in darkness…
The *Daily Mail*'s Jeff Powell, after Sven's appointment as England coach.

Both sides have scored a couple of goals and both sides have conceded a couple of goals. Peter Withe

The Anfield shrine with its long queue wrapped round the ground provokes comparison with Lenin's tomb; there is the same reverence, the same sense of a religious need fulfilled. John Sweeney describes Anfield after Hillsborough.

A penalty is a cowardly way to score. Pele, 1966.

It was one of those goals that's invariably a goal. Denis Law

In my lifetime, there have been three British footballers who would walk into St. Peter's All Time XI. They are Tom Finney, George Best and John Charles.

Michael Parkinson *Daily Telegraph* 26/02/04

All strikers go through what they call a glut, where they don't score goals. Mark Lawrenson nutmegs himself.

He was on the six-yard line, just two yards away from the goal. Pat Nevin gets tongue-tied over Henrik Larsson.

And the Liverpool goalkeeper Chris Kirkland has signed a contract which will keep him at the club until the start of the next century. Simon Brotherton, Radio 5 Live in 2001.

With eight or ten minutes to go, they were able to bring Nicky Butt back and give him fifteen to twenty minutes. Niall Quinn

With eight minutes gone, the game could be won in the next five or ten minutes. Jimmy Armfield calls it early.

He hit the post, and after the game people are going to say, well, he hit the post. **Jimmy Greaves**

They've forced them into a lot of unforced errors. Steve Claridge

I'm not going to pick out anyone in particular but Jay Jay Okocha should not be the captain of a football club. **Rodney Marsh**

That was an inch-perfect pass to no one.
Ray Wilkins

Sheffield Wednesday the winners 2-0, leaving the Anfield crowd brainwashed.
Stuart Hall

Bergkamp's just been on another plane.

Peter Drury, obviously not describing Dennis's travel arrangements.

I'd like to have seen Tony Morley left on as a down-and-out winger. Jimmy Armfield

Lord Nelson! Lord Beaverbrook! Sir Winston Churchill! Sir Anthony Eden! Clement Attlee! Henry Cooper! Lady Diana! Maggie Thatcher can you hear me? Maggie Thatcher! Your boys took a hell of a beating! Your boys took a hell of a beating! Bjorn Lillelien, Norwegian commentator, after his countrymen overcome England in a 1981 World Cup qualifier.

It's got nothing to do with his ability. In fact, it has got to do with his ability.

Barry Venison

Portsmouth are at Huddersfield, which is always away. Jimmy Greaves

He's only a foot away from the linesman, or should I say a metre in modern parlance. **Jimmy Armfield**

If you had a linesman on each side of the pitch in both halves you'd have nearly four. **Robbie Earle**

The ball could have gone anywhere and almost did. Brian Marwood

The first half was end-to-end stuff. In contrast, in this second half it's been one end to the other. Lou Macari

...and tonight we have the added ingredient of Kenny Dalglish not being here.

Martin Tyler

Glenn Hoddle

Steven Carr has hit a small blimp.

Compared to the preparation Brazil have had, we are motorways behind them, absolute motorways. Still, it's no use crying over spilt milk, we'll just have to get a new cow. What rubbish.

You can't compare two players who are different because they're not the same.

Glenn is putting his head in the frying pan.

Osvaldo Ardiles decapitates his former team-mate.

If Glenn Hoddle were any other nationality, he would have had 70 or 80 caps for England.

John Barnes

Jesus was a normal, run-of-the-mill sort of guy who had a genuine gift, just as Eileen [Drewery] has.

Thanks, Glenn.

No-one at Tottenham would shed a single tear if Glenn Hoddle was sacked tomorrow. The dressing room is not together and there is no team spirit. He has absolutely no man management skills.

Tim Sherwood fails to mince his words. *The Guardian* 22/09/03

I thought Christians were supposed to forgive people their sins but that doesn't seem to be the case with me. Chris Sutton after Hoddle refuses to pick him for England.

His tackle was definitely pre-ordained.

Michael Owen is a goalscorer, not a natural born one yet, that takes time.

He was a player that hasn't had to use his legs, even when he was nineteen years of age because his first two yards were in his head.

With hindsight, it's easy to look at it with hindsight.

If anyone is found guilty, I will step on them.

We didn't have the run of the mill.

International football is one cog further up the football ladder.

I think in international football you have to be able to handle the ball.

I have a number of alternatives and each one gives me something different.

That was the way to nail the record to the mast.

The FA Cup is still definitely the best cup in the world.

OK, we lost.
But good things
can come of it
– negative and
positive.

Not a Happy Bunny:

They call him Big Ron because he is a big spender in the transfer market. I just call him Fat Ron. Malcolm Allison, 1993.

Be careful. You're going to die tonight. Macedonia captain Artim Sakiri to David Beckham before a Euro 2004 qualifier. *Independent* quotes of the year

...stepping off the edge of the world into silence.

Chris Waddle on taking the penalty that cost England a place in the 1990 World Cup Final.

Really serious offences should not be given the name 'foul' but should be seen as what they are: criminal assaults. Osvaldo Ardiles

I think Spurs ought to buy a good stock of cotton wool for such poseurs. He can't expect not to be tackled just because Argentina won the World Cup. Tommy Smith fails to recognise the pedigree of Osvaldo Ardiles.

Terrible Senegalese Ref Robs Ghana of a Classic Goal No 3 by Tony Yeboah! **Headline from *Africa Sports* after a World Cup qualifier in 1992 between Ghana and Algeria.**

It's not as if I've dropped a nuclear bomb on them. The Americans still get in, don't they? **Maradona on discovering his dodgy drugs record had denied him automatic entry to Japan.**

Football management these days is like nuclear war: no winners, just survivors. **Tommy Docherty**

I don't like the Germans. Every time I played against German players, I had a problem because of the War. Eighty per cent of my family died in this war; my daddy, my sister, two brothers. And every game against players from Germany makes me angry. **Dutch international Wim van Hanegem explains his absence from the official banquet after the 1974 World Cup Final between Holland and West Germany. *Brilliant Orange:***

I haven't had the chance to kick a Celtic player for many years. **Ex-Rangers captain Terry Butcher relishes turning out in a veterans' Old Firm game.**

At the moment, we couldn't hit a cow's arse with a banjo. Dave Bassett is not upbeat about Sheffield United.

I did once hit a player with a dead pigeon. His name was Declan Roche and he was talking back to me, so I got these dead pigeons out of a box and slapped him with one. Partick Thistle manager John Lambie.

Why don't they put us in Division One?
Arsene Wenger gets a complex as Arsenal's disciplinary record comes up before the FA... again. *The Guardian* 26/09/03

If United fail to beat Wolves tonight, will the last person out of Elland Road please turn off the lights? Back page of the *Yorkshire Post*
before Leeds' vital relegation clash (they won 4-1). *Observer Sport magazine*, 03/04

It's been so long since we've had a penalty nobody knew who was taking it. We had forgotten where the spot was.

'Boro manager Steve McClaren bemoans his team's luck.

They need to learn a lot about manners… we certainly gave them respect, but I don't think they gave us much back. We wish them well in the FA Trophy, we hope they get beat in the next round. Newcastle boss Kenny Dalglish, after the Magpies dispose of Stevenage in an FA Cup replay.

One thing I've learned from being at Spurs is the word crisis. Gerry Francis on the manager's job at White Hart Lane.

I had to change the team three times between 10.30am and kick-off. I ended up going into the boot room and finding two kids, Anthony Pulis and Warren Hunt, having a cup of tea. I then needed another so I found Shaun Cooper, who was having a meat pie when I told him he was on the bench. Harry Redknapp despairs at Portsmouth's match-day injury crisis. *The Guardian* 07/01/04

If we lose our passion we might as well end up playing netball.
West Brom manager Gary Megson.

I always thought he was a proper player but now to me he's just another Johnny Foreigner.
Graeme Souness gets narked at the alleged playacting of Villa's Ronny Johnsen. *Times,* 31/12/03

Don't swap shirts with those dirty bastards. **Alex Ferguson on Feyenoord after a Champions League tie.**

I could see Fergie's face turning purple. "Club car?" he yelled. "You've got more chance of getting a club bike." **Ryan Giggs on how not to ask Alex Ferguson for a set of wheels.** *FourFourTwo:* 09/2002

Down to one man, Don Revie. He preferred the workhorse type of player. **Frank Worthington reflects on his lack of England appearances.**

It will take a very, very long time to sort things out. It is a rat-infested place. Outgoing City manager Frank Clark on the problems at Maine Road.

We'll train Christmas Day. I don't give a shit about Christmas. I'm going to be the most miserable person you have ever seen in your whole life. Harry Redknapp after Portsmouth's 3-0 defeat at Southampton. *The Guardian* 22/12/03

We should be going home wearing pointed hats with the word 'dopes' written on them. Graeme Souness reacts badly to a Blackburn defeat at Upton Park.

I've always said that when he's moaning, he's happy. That's a Liverpool thing, they are the world's biggest moaners. Villa boss John Gregory on Steve Staunton.

Our passing was poor, we didn't get behind the ball, but I still blame the referee. Bryan Robson finds a convenient scapegoat.

I don't blame individuals. I blame myself.
Joe Royle

He's Australian. He's in the Commonwealth. They fought the war with us. I know that might sound like b*ll*cks to you but we let foreign people in who have no allegiance to this country. **Harry Redknapp goes over the top after Hayden Foxe's work permit gets delayed.**

I didn't know you were a Spurs fan.
Blackburn boss Graeme Souness to referee Graham Poll. *The Guardian* 24/12/03

I shouldn't say what I really feel, but Poll was their best midfielder. You saw him coming off at half-time and he smiled so much he obviously enjoyed that performance. **Sheffield United manager Neil Warnock suggests referee Graham Poll is a gooner, after the Blades' FA Cup semi-final v Arsenal, 2003.**

I know I have been banned for talking about officials, but these days referees have got no bottle – and I thought the linesman was pathetic.
Joe Kinnear

It looked as if we'd picked eleven people off the streets of Birmingham and asked them if they wanted a game.

Birmingham boss Steve Bruce bemoans an FA Cup exit at the hands of Sunderland. *Daily Telegraph* 26/02/04

All of us would say 'great player, decent manager', but as man we wouldn't have anything to add. Walking down the corridor in the morning, he wouldn't even say hello.

The departing Keith Gillespie on Blackburn boss Graeme Souness.

There was nothing pleasurable to think about or remember.

Bolton boss Sam Allardyce after the 2004 Carling Cup Final defeat to Middlesbrough. *The Guardian* 01/03/04

Our best football will come against the right type of opposition. A team who come to play football and not act as animals. Sir Alf Ramsey

is incensed by Argentina's tactics during the 1966 World Cup quarter-final against England.

If I wasn't the manager
I'd have gone home early.

Hibs manager Alex Miller watches his team's nil-nil.

Stick with that guy and you'll get relegated. Mark Viduka to his Leeds team-mates after a spat with then manager Peter Reid... allegedly. *The Guardian* 11/11/03

It was like asking Frank Sinatra to sing in front of three-dozen people! Jimmy Greaves on playing to small crowds at the 1962 World Cup finals.

Everyone knows that for us to get a penalty we need a certificate from the Pope and a personal letter from the Queen. Alex Ferguson answers criticism that United get more than their fair share.

People have got this preconceived idea of me as a fat bastard who can't move. Andy Goram bites back.

My life would have ended then if I had gone through with the plan that leapt into my mind: to drive my car at maximum speed and crash.

Nobby Stiles on depression following his playing career.

There have been a few defenders who have come and left because I have been in their position, and bigger names than Steve Finnan. Jamie Carragher extends a warm welcome to the incoming Steve Finnan.

The manager brought in a psychologist to help us through the troubled times. Those who wanted help or who were feeling more fragile could talk to the psychologist when they wanted to. Stephane Henchoz

I'll not go to the f*****g World Cup. Now you can have your excuse. It's all Roy's fault. See ye later, lads.

Niall Quinn recounts Roy Keane's parting shot before storming out of the 2002 World Cup finals.

You are filth and you smell of manure…

Belgian coach Robert Waseige loses it with his country's press at the 2002 World Cup.

You scored the goal that wasn't a goal.

Franz Beckenbauer to Geoff Hurst, sixteen years after 1966.

My main doubt is whether he has the sufficient greatness as a person to justify being honoured by a worldwide audience. Pele is peeved after Maradona beats him into second place in FIFA's player of the century poll.

At the end of the match, Bilic came to apologise. He knew he'd deprived me of the Final. And I thought "Maybe I should hit him now". Laurent Blanc on Slaven Bilic, whose playacting in the 1998 World Cup semi-final caused Blanc's dismissal.

The Beatles are a good example. In the beginning, like them, we had enthusiasm together. But later the pleasure was gone, we didn't want to play together any more.

Former Ajax midfielder Gerrie Muhren on the break-up of the legendary Seventies' team. *Brilliant Orange:*

We've been playing for an hour and it's just occurred to me that we re drawing 0-0 with a mountain top.

Scottish radio commentator Ian Archer despairs of his team's performance against San Marino.

I have come to accept that the life of a front-runner is a hard one, that he will suffer more injuries that most men and that many of those injuries will not be accidental. Pele

When an African team takes place in a tournament like this, the players are always asked two questions by foreign journalists: "Do you have a witch doctor?" and "Do you eat monkeys?"

Cameroon's Francois Omam Biyick at the 1990 World Cup finals.

I hope to God they don't become footballers. I hope I die first.
Dulcie Summerbee, husband of George, mother of Mike and grandmother of Nicky, hopes her great-grandchildren don't catch the bug.

They used to boo me before we'd even kicked off – 'Number seven Nicky Summerbee' and they all booed. That's great for your confidence, isn't it?
Nicky Summerbee on failing to win over the Maine Road faithful.

In future, I will never allow anybody in this country to operate on me with a knife and fork.
Steffen Iverson suggests that Tottenham's medical staff are less than first-rate.

The specialist did these tests, pulled the leg every way imaginable and then took some x-rays. After lengthy analysis he told me, "Your knee is f**ked". Julian Dicks gets blinded with science.

We've just lost to the hatchet men of Panathinaikos in the first leg of our UEFA Cup-tie. To say it was rough would be like saying that Everest is a pretty big hill. **Ian Rush recalls Juventus v Panathinaikos ruefully.**

He ought to be done away with, it's a shame he hasn't been topped before. Leicester's Dave Bassett leads the lynch mob against Spurs defender Taricco.

A few years ago, the Queen talked about her annus horriblis. I didn't know what it meant at the time, but I do now. **Alan Shearer on a rare lean season.**

I knew malaria would have to set in before I would get a game under Lawrie. We had a good working relationship. He stayed away from the training ground – and I was chuffed. **Jim Magilton on Lawrie McMenemy.**

They sold me like a cow. Jaap Stam bears a grudge after leaving Manchester United for Lazio.

I didn't get many scoring chances at Forest. I'd rather kill myself than go through that again. **Pierre van Hooijdonk**

I think it is a betrayal of our heritage, of our culture and of the structure of the game in this country.

PFA boss Gordon Taylor takes issue with the FA's appointment of Sven.

I will never go back to Scotland again, even when I'm dead. **Marco Negri fails to heal the rift at Ibrox.**

Hartson's got more previous than Jack the Ripper.

Harry Redknapp

Come near me son and I'll break your back. **Ex-Liverpool defender Tommy Smith's self-confessed warning to opposing forwards.**

Basically, I'm a nasty little guy because I always want to win. If I have to boot someone, I'll boot them, simple as that. **Dennis Wise**

Dennis Wise has made a living out of being a cheat… Dennis tries to be your mate all the time but he quickly forgets that's he's just kicked you in the head, two-footed you or stuck his finger in your ear.

Jason McAteer removes Dennis Wise from his Christmas card list. *The Sun* 19/01/04

Somebody would give him the ball and I'd make a run to collect it in the box and it would never arrive. I'd turn around and he'd be juggling it like a bloody seal. Manchester City's Neil Young on Rodney Marsh. *Observer Sport Monthly.*

It's just like playing alongside Barbara Streisand.
Mike Summerbee on the showmanship of Rodney Marsh, 1973.

If I was playing in red it would have been a certain penalty. It's probably too much for me to win one at Old Trafford in front of the Stretford End, isn't it?
Alan Shearer bemoans his fate after being tripped by United's Tim Howard.
The Guardian 19/01/04

If Liverpool hadn't won all those league titles years ago and then we'd won that treble, we'd be legends forever. Jamie Carragher
inflates the importance of Liverpool's three cups in 2001. *The Guardian* 24/01/04

It was like playing people from outer space.
England defender Syd Owen on playing Hungary's 'mighty Magyars' of the 1950s.

I came away wondering to myself what we had been doing all these years.
England's Tom Finney after the famous 6-3 drubbing by Hungary at Wembley in 1953.

You are an Englishman.
German captain Franz Beckenbauer to referee Jack Taylor at the 1974 World Cup Final, after Taylor had awarded Holland a first-minute penalty.
Brilliant Orange:

Stalingrad.

Explanation from Azerbaijani linesman Tofik Bakhramov as to why he gave England's third, 'on-the-line' goal at the 1966 World Cup Final.

There is a mafia even in the soccer world. The penalty didn't exist. It was given to let the Germans win. Diego Maradona spits sour grapes after the 1990 World Cup Final.

He stuck his head in and went down holding his face to get me sent off. I'd rather he'd have kicked me than do that. He's a cheat. Leicester's Paul Dickov accuses Alex Rae of Wolves. *The Guardian* 01/03/04

I feel ashamed for myself and Scotland, but I do not think that some of the Scottish team have the brains to feel ashamed. Martin Buchan, after Scotland took one point from Peru and Iran at the 1978 World Cup finals.

It was one you could stop without arms and legs. The self-loathing of Bayern keeper Oliver Kahn, after handing Real Madrid a soft goal in the Champions League. *Observer* 07/03/04

What's the point of being the best player in the world if I am not happy? Maradona's question to God in Maradona: The Musical, which opened in Buenos Aires in January 2004. *Observer Sport magazine,* 03/2004

It's a mixture of feeling sick and wanting to cry at the same time. Lawrie McMenemy describes the taste of defeat.

I don't blame Chris. I don't blame anyone but myself. It was my fault that England were not in the World Cup Final. Stuart Pearce on missing that penalty in Turin.

As one door closes, another one shuts.
Howard Wilkinson

Take Ruud Gullit. I never liked his arrogance. In fact, I never liked him, but while he was delivering the goods there was no problem. When he lost the plot, he had to go. Ken Bates, former Chelsea chairman.

It takes one to know one. I'm surprised Martin O'Neill knows as big a word as cretin.
Ken Bates goes back to the playground.

He is one of the most jealous people I have ever seen. I gave him a slap because I could not stand it any more. Eyal Berkovic on team-mate John Moncur.

We were caviar in the first half, cabbage in the second. Phil Thompson on a Jeckyll-and-Hyde display by Liverpool at Charlton.

It was like facing the Harlem Globetrotters.

Gary Neville describes playing against Real Madrid. *Time*, 31/12/03

Even if Tom Finney had played at his age he would have had a good game against us.

Palace manager Alan Smith is unimpressed by his team's defeat at Preston.

These agents get you over to see this fantastic striker you can take on loan, you get there and he's on the bench. On Friday I'm stood outside a hotel in Alaves at four o'clock in the morning, pissing down with rain… I thought to myself "I wonder if Arsene Wenger or Alex Ferguson would be stood outside this hotel at 4am in Alaves? What am I doing?" Harry Redknapp on his desperate search for a new striker. *The Guardian* 26/01/04

I lay in bed the other night thinking about strikers. It's a few years ago now but I can remember there were always much better things to do in bed.

Harry Redknapp keeps his mind on the job. *Nuts*

I know I'm going to get slaughtered.
Gerard Houllier sees the gathering storm after Liverpool's FA Cup exit at Portsmouth. *The Guardian* 23/02/04

We will have to win the League now after failing in Europe or we will all be shot.
Steve McManaman on the price of failure at Real Madrid.

The stupid, bloody rule. Is he offside or not? We don't know what to do with it. You can't coach against it. It's rubbish. **Wolves manager David Jones speaks for all of us as the offside law becomes more nonsensical.** *The Guardian* 09/02/04

The last time we got a penalty away from home, Christ was a carpenter. **Lennie Lawrence suspects a conspiracy against Charlton, 1989.**

I have this book with two players' names in it. If I get the chance to do them, I will. I'll make them suffer before I pack it in. If I can kick them four yards over the touchline, I will.

Jack Charlton on his notorious 'little black book'

I don't know how it could have happened. I can't imagine him jumping for a ball. I think one of his eyelashes must have come out... I wouldn't know if he was match fit, I've never seen him fit. George Graham on a head wound sustained by Palace's Thomas Brolin.

I'm thinking of suing Glenn Hoddle for compensation for missing my holiday. I paid £1,024 for it, and I won't be getting my money back. I even bought a travel iron.

Paul Gascoigne's dad after his son is omitted from the 1998 World Cup squad.

Dear Dad,

I hope you don't mind but I don't want to be a Spurs fan any more.

Love
Sam

Letter from nine-year-old Sam Curtis to journalist father Adrian, after Spurs surrendered a 3-0 half-time lead to Manchester City in an FA Cup replay. *The Evening Standard,* 05/02/04

Football makes me emotional. Not many people can explain what it's like when you play all season and you get to Wembley or somewhere, and at the end you and all the lads walk down the tunnel while the other lot are doing the lap of honour.

Norman Hunter on some nearly days at Leeds.

Sir Bobby Robson

Guppy has a dextrous left foot.

Manchester United will find it very intimidating with 100 screaming fans in the Bernabeu.

We had ten times as many shots on target as Bolton, and they had none at all... Robson fails the maths.

The first 90 minutes are the most important.

I'm not going to look beyond the semi-final, but I would love to lead Newcastle out at the Final.

In a year's time, he's a year older.

Denis once kicked me at Wembley in front of the Queen in an international. I mean, no man is entitled to do that, really. **Bobby gets miffed about Denis Law.**

Jermaine Jenas is a fit lad. He gets from box to box in all of 90 minutes.

Well, I don't know if I'm going to live to be 127. **On being asked if he would remain Newcastle's manager until they won something.** *The Guardian* 24/01/04

I'm glad we don't have to play them every week. Oh, we've got them again on Saturday in the FA Cup. **After a Newcastle defeat by Arsenal.**

Ray Wilkins' day will come one night

There will be a game where somebody scores more than Brazil and that might be the game that they lose.

Maybe not goodbye, but farewell.

Home advantage gives you an advantage.

Eighteen months ago they [Sweden] were arguably one of the best three teams in Europe, and that would include Germany, Holland, Russia and anybody else if you like.

If we starting counting our chickens before they hatch, they won't lay any eggs in the basket.

Where do you get an experienced player like him with a left foot and a head?

Gary Speed has never played better,
never looked fitter, never been older.

He [Sir Bobby Robson] is only
six months older than he was
last season. **Alan Shearer does the math.** *The Guardian* 06/09/03

His influence on the team through his personality
and playing ability cannot be underestimated.

I thought that individually and as
a pair, they'd do better together.

That's easy. On Saturday afternoon, Viana;
Saturday night, Viagra. On selection and scoring.

They've probably played better than they've ever done for a few weeks.

Some of the goals were good, some of the goals were sceptical.

The margin is very marginal.

We've got nothing to lose, and there is no point losing this game.

He's got his legs back, of course, or his leg. He's always had one but now he's got two.

Everyone's got tough games coming up. Manchester United have got Arsenal, Arsenal have got Manchester United and Leeds have got Leeds.

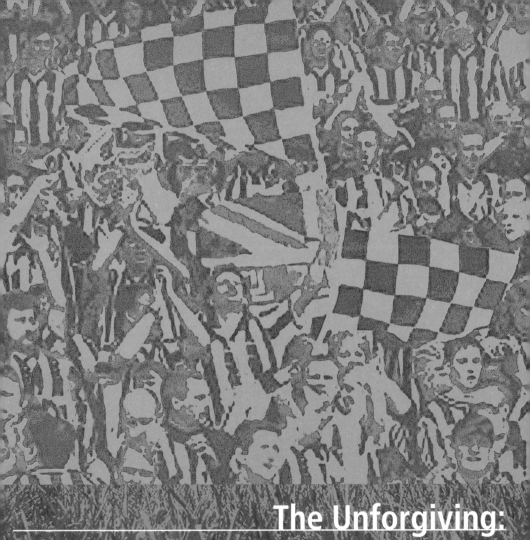

The Unforgiving:

He's fat, he's round, he's never in the ground, Captain Bob.
Oxford (and Derby) fans' question the attendance record of chairman Robert Maxwell.

George, the rabbi wants the ball! Give it 'im!
Wag in the Fulham crowd suggests George Cohen passes to Jimmy Hill.

Lenny is a large man sporting a large and frequently unveiled stomach and carrying a briefcase which contains a large pie, presented to raucous cheers from supporters before each game. Description of unofficial Bradford City mascot Lennie, the City Gent, on fans' website Boys from Brazil.

Two pints of Theakstons, a bowl of pie & peas and a cigar... and still change from a fiver!
A seal of approval from a Gillingham fan, drinking in Burnley before a match at Turf Moor.

Do the Ayatollah!
Cardiff City chant in reverence of chairman Sam Hammam (slapping top of head whilst singing is obligatory).

The sky is blue, the clouds are white, God must be a Spireite!
Chesterfield

I can't read and I can't write, it doesn't really matter.
'Cos I come from Hertfordshire, and I can drive a tractor.
Watford

Never felt more like swinging a pig, from Hyde Park flats, to Wadsley Bridge, U-ni-ted! You ve got me swinging a pig! Sheffield United fans sing of a local custom.

Oh fluffy sheep, are wonderful, oh fluffy sheep are wonderful. Because they're white and they're Welsh, oh fluffy sheep are wonderful. Wrexham fans bask in the stereotype.

Juve! It's just like watching Juve!

Notts County (Juventus adopted County's black and white stripes when the club was formed by Englishmen at the beginning of the last century).

Sing when we're fishing, we only sing when we're fishing.
Grimsby fans pay tribute to the local industry.

Ooo arrr! It's Ambrrrosia!

Plymouth fans declare their love for creamed rice pudding.

When they start singing 'You'll Never Walk Alone', my eyes start to water. There have been times when I've actually been crying while I've been playing. Kevin Keegan on the emotion generated from the Kop.

I would rather gouge my eyes out with a rusty spoon than have O'Leary back. Simon Jose of Leeds United Independent Fans' Association, casts his negative vote. *Independent* quotes of the year

Greedy board, weak manager, mug fans.

A West Ham fan sums up the state of the club following relegation. *Times*, 31/12/03

Sort it out Houllier. Not good enough for Liverpool Football Club. No more expensive mistakes. We want the title! Banner unveiled at Anfield says it all. *Observer* 25/01/04

Manchester United fans can be found in all walks of life. They may smile at you in newsagents' shops or in bus queues. You can find them on parent-teacher associations or in local amateur dramatic societies. They will not be found in the environs of Manchester. Colin Schindler, Manchester City fan, gets it wrong

When Rioch came to Millwall we were depressed and miserable. He's done a brilliant job of turning it all around. Now we're miserable and depressed. Danny Baker on BBC Radio 5 Live's 606.

Although French stadia are more modern, they are used for other things such as athletics. But I prefer British stadia. I prefer the atmosphere here. You are closer to the public. It is warmer, there is room for love.
Eric prefers Portman Road to the Parc des Princes.

You're getting sacked in the summer.
Charlton fans to Claudio Ranieri. *The Guardian* 09/02/04

1995 was a great year for English football. Eric was banned.
T-shirt slogan and variation on the Nike advertising campaign.

If you can imagine spending five years with an overgrown child clambering about in your attic, then you'll have a fair idea of the impact Graeme Souness has made on Scottish football.
When Saturday Comes writer Graham McColl assesses Souness's tenure at Ibrox.

We dream of playing in the shirt. Today God chose you. Play like the dream. Banner at the City of Manchester stadium during the home team's mid-season slump. *The Guardian* 09/02/04

Beans. Cobi Jones just can't get used to them. Forget the weather, the TV, the accents, the psychopathic full-backs paying him close attention on the mud-laden pitches of the West Midlands. It's the humble products of Heinz, Crosse & Blackwell et al that are causing him real problems. *90 Minutes* cultural difference facing an American at Coventry.

Can we play you every week?

Portsmouth fans show a sense of humour at 5-0 down to Arsenal in an FA Cup quarter-final. *Observer* 07/03/04

Turnip's going up! Watford fans' take on Graham Taylor leading them to promotion.

You don't understand Newcastle United until you understand the hero wears the number 9 shirt. Cardinal Basil Hulme is a fan.

He's got a pineapple – on his head. Ubiquitous chant at Jason Lee, owing to his unique hairstyle.

I used to stand up and glare around when fans were giving Geoff stick and they all used to shout, 'Wasn't me Mrs Hurstie, wasn't me'.

Geoff Hurst's mother takes on the ICF.

I was in the Leeds end, chanting and going mad, and the fans were saying 'Hold on, what's he doing here?'

Noel Whelan on playing for and supporting Leeds.

If I had to pack the game in tomorrow, I would go straight out and buy a season ticket for Maine Road... I grew up in a town that only wanted to know Manchester United and I've been lucky enough to change that.

City legend Mike Doyle.

Joe Jordan strikes quicker than British Leyland. **1970s Scottish banner at Wembley.**

Off you go, Cantona. It's an early bath for you.

Palace fan Matthew Simmons' own unlikely version of his verbal assault on Eric Cantona, which led to the Frenchman's infamous 'kung-fu' assault.

I looked at the fans and they were singing my name and it made me cry.

Gazza on the moment in Italia 90 when his eyes watered.
Observer Sport Monthly

Cry in a minute, he's going to cry in a minute.

Most opposition crowds to Paul Gascoigne after Italia 90.

There Ain't Nothing Like a James!

Early Highbury chant about 'Thirties legend Alex James.

We're supposed to be at home.

Brighton fans at the Priestfield Stadium after being forced to play their home games at Gillingham.

116 years of tradition ended. Message on wreath delivered by those unwilling to accept Rangers' signing of the Catholic Maurice Johnston.

All I Want for Christmas is a Dukla Prague Away Kit

Title of 1986 single from Half Man Half Biscuit.

We've lost that Terry Phelan, ohhh-woh Terry Phelan. We've lost that Terry Phelan, now it's Vonk, Vonk, Vonk.

Manchester City fans take a huge liberty with the Walker Brothers as Terry Phelan is replaced by Michael Vonk.

Man offers marriage proposal to any woman with ticket for Leeds United v Sheffield United game. Must send photograph (of ticket).

Advert placed in the *Yorkshire Evening Post* before a vital Second Division clash in 1990.

Communism v Alcoholism

Caledonian banner at the USSR v Scotland game in the 1982 World Cup finals.

Phil Neville should have his passport confiscated and not be allowed to leave the country. England fan Scott Vessey after Neville's concession of a late penalty knocks England out of Euro 2000.

We hate you so much because we loved you so much. Barcelona banner on Luis Figo's first game at the Nou Camp after transferring to Real Madrid. *Observer Sport Monthly* 01/2004

Never again fascism! Never again war! Never again Third Division! The fans from Hamburg outfit St. Pauli get their priorities right.

Liverpool – 30 miles from greatness
Visiting Man United fans unveil a banner at Anfield *The Guardian* 10/11/03

Who let the Frogs out?

Chant from Bradford City fans at Chelsea's Frank LeBoeuf.

I reckon 80 per cent of United fans don't support England. You wouldn't take a flag of St George to United. You might get confronted. Richard Kurt, deputy editor of Manchester United fanzine *Red Issue*. *Observer* 12/10/03

Piss in a bottle, you couldn't piss in a bottle.

Spurs fans to Rio Ferdinand after the United defender's eight-month ban for missing a drug test. *The Guardian* 22/12/03

Sun shining. Cheap beer. Got tickets.
See you in Istanbul. Diehard England fans.

Postcard to the FA from fans in Macedonia, poking fun at the attempted ticket ban from their own national association. *Times*, 31/12/03

Bjorn-e-bee in my gang, my gang, my gang

Reprise of the Gary Glitter tune by Blackburn fans to Stig Inge Bjornebye.

Boing! Boing! Baggies! Baggies!

West Bromwich Albion anthem.

Donkey won the derby!

Arsenal fans' chant after Tony Adams scored the winner against Spurs.

Shareholders of the World, United takeover.

Chant at Old Trafford, presumably with apologies to The Smiths. *The Guardian* 02/02/04

I was given shirt number 50 at the start of the season. They thought it was a safe one to allocate but new signing Nikos Dabizas has taken Micky Adams' squad to 44. So, if he makes five more signings, I'll be in the reckoning and could get a game. **Leicester City mascot Filbert Fox.** *The Guardian* 19/01/04

Timmy Tourettes, he's in our nets, f**k off, f**k off, f**k off.

Man United fans laud 'keeper Tim Howard, a victim of Tourette Syndrome. *Observer* 24/08/03

One of the only other high points of the season was hoodwinking our beloved neighbours into taking the woeful Abel Xavier off our hands AND paying us half a million pounds for the privilege!

Mark Staniford from Everton fanzine *Speke from the Harbour*.

Live round the corner, you only live round the corner.

Universal chant to Manchester United away fans.

He's fat, he's round, his car is in the pound, Jan Molby.

Variation on a theme after Liverpool's midfielder failed the breathalyser.

Come in a taxi, you must have come in a taxi.

Sung to any small groups of away fans. Various

Liam Brady lays on more balls than Susan George.

Arsenal banner at one of their late-'70s Cup Finals.

Subbuteo! You're having a laugh.

Old Trafford taunt to Rangers fans during a Champions League humiliation.

One Mrs Zola, there's only one Mrs Zola.

Chelsea fans thank Gianfranco's spouse after she reportedly persuaded hubby to stay at Stamford Bridge for another season.

Who put the ball in the Scousers' net? Jerzy, Jerzy Dudek.

The red half of Manchester celebrates a goalkeeping present.

Channel 5, Channel 5, Channel 5.

Arsenal fans point out to Liverpool rivals that they are in the UEFA Cup, not the Champions League.

Eight men will never play again, who met destruction there, The flowers of English football, the flowers of Manchester.

Poem written to those who died at the Munich air disaster.

Give us back our bicycles.

Dutch chant against Germany during Euro '88, a reference to the Nazis' mass confiscation of the nation's bikes during World War II. *Brilliant Orange:*

Shall we buy a crowd for you?

Visiting Chelsea fans suggest that Highbury is a tad quiet.

You can't see your willy, you can't see your willy, la la la la.
A Stamford Bridge chorus to a rotund Oxford goalkeeper.

Woolwich rejects.
Charlton taunt to former South Londoners Arsenal.

Flats on the Cottage, they're building flats on the Cottage.
Aimed at Fulham fans since their departure to Loftus Road.

Small club in Moscow, you're just a small club in Moscow. Bolton fans sniff at Chelsea's nouveau riche.

Tell me ma, me ma, To put the champagne on ice, We're going to Wembley twice. Everton fans murder Doris Day during a particularly good cup season.

Sit down Pinocchio!
To Phil Thompson whenever he leaves the dugout.

The Dave Bassett season! Big white false teeth, big white false smile, promises that could never be kept and about 2p left in the kitty.
Gary Silke of Leicester's *The Fox* fanzine on Dave Bassett's tenure at Filbert Street.

We are Millwall, we are Millwall, no-one likes us, we don't care. **Lions' fans adopt a spot of self-analysis.**

Georgie Best, superstar. Walks like a woman and he wears a bra.

Early example of derogatory chant.

Kick it off, throw it in, have a little scrimmage, Keep it low, splendid rush, bravo, win or die. **Start of curious and quaint chant still sung at Carrow Road.**

He was laughable, waddling around at a pace barely discernible from a stroll in a manner that suggested some fat geezer who'd won a 'Play a Match with the Hornets' raffle. **Fan Ian Grant describes the four-game career of Mick Quinn.**

David James, superstar, drops more b*****ks than Grobelaar. **Manchester United fans at Anfield.**

Have you got another kit?

Southampton fans bait Manchester United, one season after Fergie had blamed their defeat on the apparent camouflageable quality of a new grey strip.

I am disgusted. And, if Hoddle is the new manager, I will be taking my season ticket and my son's back to the ground along with our club shirts. A Forest fan vents his anger after Paul Hart is fired as manager at Nottingham Forest. *The Guardian* 09/02.04

An uninterrupted view of Norway.

Disgruntled Chelsea fan on the view from the top tier at Newcastle's St.James's Park.

If you've all got a passport clap your hands. Sung to Mohammad Al Fayed while waving British passport above head.

Are you Vale in disguise?

England's Stoke City contingent bestow the 'ultimate insult' on Argentina at the 2002 World Cup.

The first time I got the ball for a throw-in the fans were all shouting at me "What have you done to your hair?" Chris Waddle on the first appearance of his infamous mullet.

One team in Tallinn. There's only one team in Tallinn.

Scottish fans at the World Cup qualifier in Estonia. After a protest over the kick-off time, Scotland kicked off against no opposition.

Gordon Strachan

It's a tremendous honour. I'm going to have a banana to celebrate. On being voted Footballer of the Year in 1991.

I don't know how you face people after that. When you go and speak to your mates and they ask what did you contribute to the game and you say "I fell, I fell like a big Jessie". Gordon pours scorn on the antics of Bolton's Mario Jardel. *Independent* quotes of the year

I just told them – it's not your pitch anyway. Aside to Fulham fans after straying from the technical area at Loftus Road.

I'm just hoping Robbie doesn't like the San Siro, doesn't like the wages and wants to come back here. As Coventry manager, after Robbie Keane's transfer to Inter Milan.

We'll try and win because we're not clever enough to try anything else. **Before Southampton's UEFA Cup tie against Steaua Bucharest.** *Times,* 31/12/03

You could smell the fear in my players in the first 45 minutes – I've never seen that before, no matter who we've played. We've always had the stomach for the fight, but it wasn't there. You can't live life with fear like that, never mind football. **Gordon condemns his Southampton team's approach against Arsenal.** *Independent* 03/01/04

I used to talk to the ref but it is easier to see the Pope. If I'm in London next time and I get mugged I hope the same amount of people turn up – there were six police officers, four stewards and a United Nations peace-keeping observer. **After a Southampton home defeat.** *Independent* 14/02/04

I've told him there is always room for bald, grumpy old men in my team. **On Saints midfielder Chris Marsden.**

I've taken a pay cut to come here.
As long as the fridge is full, I'm happy.
On arriving at Coventry in 1995.

I can never sell him because the other players'
wives, the manager's wife and the coach's wife
will all be up in the arms. Strachan suggests James Beattie is
something of a pin-up.

That'll be the Samaritans.
They usually call me this
time of day. After a mobile going off at a Southampton
post-match press conference.

Apart from yourself, we're all quite positive round
here. I'm going to whack you over the head with
a big stick. Down, negative man, down.
To another hapless reporter.

We're not doing bad. What do you expect us to be like? We were eighth in the league last year, in the Cup Final and we got into Europe. I don't know where you expect me to get to. Do you expect us to win the Champions League? Gordon is peeved after a reporter's careless question.

There's nobody fitter at his age, except perhaps Raquel Welch. Praise for Gordon's fitness from Big Ron.

The leg is out of the coffin now and if we can get anything at Old Trafford next weekend, then we will have two legs out. On Coventry's attempted escapology from the relegation zone.

I've got more important things to think about. I've got a yoghourt to finish by today. The expiry date is today. That can be my priority rather than Austin Delgado. Gordon's plan of action.

No, I'm just going to crumble like a wreck. I'll go home, become an alcoholic and maybe jump off a bridge. On being asked whether he could take the pressure.

No. I was asked whether I thought I was the right man for the job and I said 'No. I think they should have got George Graham because I'm useless'.

I don't know. I'll have to see where Easyjet are going.

Gordon's travel plans remained hazy following his departure from St. Mary's.
The Guardian 09/02/04

He never shuts up. Talks some rubbish, but we throw that away and sometimes intelligence comes out. Gordon as Coventry manager on Carlton Palmer.

Minging.

Gordon's verdict on
Bolton 0 Southampton 0.
The Guardian 10/11/03

You're right.
It is a daft question.
I'm not even going
to bother answering
that one. You're
spot on there.

Not So Stupid After All:

It would have been an insult to myself.

Bobby Moore, on suggestions that he should have kicked Pele during their classic World Cup encounter.

I don't really mind that I'm only remembered as a bloke who went in hard. It's better than not being remembered at all. Ron 'Chopper' Harris in his autobiography.

This is Britain in the 1990s. A Labour-supporting multi-millionaire who liked a beer with the lads and put his wealth into football seems like an authentic hero. Matthew Engel in *The Guardian* questions the myth surrounding the late Chelsea director Matthew Harding.

In the course of time it will be said that Maradona was to football what Rimbaud was to poetry and Mozart to music.
Eric Cantona

The world in which we live is boring. If you're different, you're considered crazy. Eric Cantona

Imagine Franz Beckenbauer trying to play for Watford. He'd just be in the way.

Frank McLintock disdains Graham Taylor's long-ball approach, 1982.

You'll never meet Des Walker.

Journalists' running gag. Des was not known for talking to the press.

You could hardly be worse off sitting on your food and eating your seat. The nutritional value could not be any lower, nor the view any worse. **Colman's Football Food Guide delivers its verdict on Wembley.**

MADR.I.P.

Headline in 1999 from Catalan's *Sport*, following Real Madrid's elimination from the Champions League.

Thank goodness at least one member of the Hill family knows something about football!

Gary Lineker reviews the footie-based novel, *Penalty Chick*, by Jimmy Hill's wife Bryony. Jacket review

Fenerbahce's Saracoglu stadium, a ground with more flares than a Showaddywaddy convention. The Observer's take on a tendency for the volatile in Turkey. *Observer Sport Monthly*

Batty would probably get himself booked playing Handel's Largo. David Lacey in *The Guardian*.

Footballers have a very short career… a few seasons in the spotlight is followed by retirement, death and then a stint on Sky Soccer Saturday. **Jeff Stelling, host of Sky Soccer Saturday, attempts not to get his contract renewed.** *Nuts*

The only person, who, when he appears on television, makes daleks hide behind the sofa. **Peter Beardsley described in the** *Observer Sport Monthly*.

The only ground that looks the same in black and white as it does in colour.
David Lacey of the *The Guardian* describes Hampden Park.

Until you've seen a match in Tegucigapla your soccer education isn't complete. The atmosphere in the stadium makes the Kop seem like a meeting of the noise-abatement society.
Chris Davies of the *Observer* describes a World Cup qualifier between Mexico and Honduras.

Why didn't you just belt it, son?
Gareth Southgate's mother offers coaching tips after her son's penalty miss at Euro '96.

As a land mass, Luxembourg might best be described as 'pert'… home advantage counts for little, when corners have to be taken from well inside Belgium.
When Saturday Comes writer Andy Lyons explains the Duchy's footballing shortcomings.

Sheedy was sent off, apparently for accusing the referee of vaginal duplicity.

The Guardian notes Kevin Sheedy's sending-off during a Chelsea v Everton cup-tie.

I just opened the trophy cabinet. Two Japanese prisoners of war fell out.
Tommy Docherty.

Apparently he finds the yellow and red a little too gaudy – which is pretty rich coming from someone who used to arrive on stage wearing a pink mohair jockstrap and a pair of angel's wings.

Journalist Giles Smith on Elton John's dislike of a new Watford kit.

Tuning into Radio 5 Live to listen to the football, there is nothing worse than having to endure reports from rugby matches… I am not the only one who wants to jail football fans who sing Swing Low Sweet Chariot. *When Saturday Comes* contributor Ken Sproat speaks for armchair fans everywhere.

If, as every Englishman suspects, the Scots ingest a weakness for hyperbole with their mother's milk, Ally MacLeod would seem to have been breast-fed until he was fifteen. **Hugh McIlvanney searches for explanations following Scotland's failed 1978 World Cup campaign.**

That's great. Tell him he's Pele and get him back on.

Partick boss John Lambie, after discovering that dazed striker Colin McGlashan did not know who he was.

It's a rat race, and the rats are winning.

Tommy Docherty

Stamford Bridge is fantastic... for potatoes.

Claudio Ranieri after Chelsea's pitch cuts up rough.

I would buy some bad players, get the sack and then retire to Cornwall. **Sheffield United boss Neil Warnock considers if he was manager of Sheffield Wednesday.**

Half a million for Remi Moses? You could get the original Moses and the tablets for that price! **Tommy Docherty disapproves of goings-on at his former club.**

I would like to thank Scotland and Mr McLeod for the team they presented us with. Peru manager, Marcos Calderon, with a nod to Ally's team selection in the 1978 World Cup Finals.

Ask me who is the best right-back in Brazil and I'll say Pele. Ask me about the best left back or the best midfield man, or the best winger, or the best centre-forward... if he wants to be the best goalkeeper, he will be. There is only one Pele. Former Brazil coach Jose Saldanha.

Brains? There's a lot of players who think manual labour is the Spanish president.
Tommy Docherty runs through the after-dinner routine.

We've watched them twice, and seen a few videos. I didn't see them 38 times though, like McCarthy says he watched us. I don't think that's possible. I did my maths you see. That's 38 times 90 minutes – that's two months and the draw was only three weeks ago. Belgium boss Georges Leekens tells his Irish counterpart Mick McCarthy to pull the other one.

I love horses, but only workhorses.

Arsene Wenger's backhanded comment on Fergie's local difficulty with Rock of Gibraltar. *The Guardian* 07/02/04

There is one, but the best manager in the world is there and he isn't giving up yet.

Martin O'Neill's candid reply to the question at his first press conference for Celtic, "Is there any othe club you would have left Leicester for?"

He's a tree surgeon who once had to have his arm sewn back on, so facing Thierry Henry won't faze him. Farnborough manager Graham Westley on defender Nathan Bunce, after drawing Arsenal in the FA Cup. *Independent* quotes of year

There was nothing between the teams apart from seven goals.

Barnsley boss Danny Wilson has tongue in cheek after a mauling at Old Trafford.

We reckon he [Carlton Palmer] covers every blade of grass on the pitch, mainly because his first touch is crap. David Jones

---

The first thing I will do is negotiate a pay rise, give myself a ten-year contract, and then sack myself. Graham Turner on the perks of owning and managing Hereford United.

It'll never replace plastic.

Ray Harford, whose QPR team played on an artificial surface, is unimpressed with the real thing.

The keeper was coming out in installments.
Joe Royle

We rode our luck, but that's what the goalposts are there for. Joe Kinnear

Oh, I dunno. I've just won a championship last year and just knocked Liverpool out. It's terrible. It's been awful. The chairman should get rid of me. Harry Redknapp can afford to joke after Portsmouth knock Liverpool out of the FA Cup. *The Guardian* 23/02/04

I've had more clubs than Jack Nicklaus.
Tommy Docherty

If I walked on water, my accusers would say it is because I can't swim.

Berti Vogts

I've been called a sadist, a sergeant major, a Glasgow tough who lashes his players. I'm not in the game to make friends. I don't want to be Tommy Docherty the popular manager. I want to be Tommy Docherty the success.
Tommy Docherty

I'm not giving secrets like that to Milan. If I had my way I wouldn't even tell them the time of the kick-off.

Bill Shankly, on being asked before a European Cup semi-final whether he was changing his team.

My team-mates advised me to visit the city first. I went to have a look at Middlesbrough and decided I was better off in Parma. Antonio Benarrivo avoids the culture shock.

You'll have to stop writing about the bleedin' figures and concentrate on the football now. But, before you do, having picked up five points from the previous fifteen games, that's six points from four undefeated since I arrived. New Forest boss Joe Kinnear spells out his early form at a press conference. *The Guardian* 01/03/04

An offence against the dignity of work.

Vatican statement on Milan's payment of £13m to Torino for Gianluigi Lentini. *Observer Sport Monthly*

Congratulations for buying Ronaldo? Thanks, but my grandma could have discovered a talent like that.
Frank Arnesen on bringing Ronaldo to PSV Eindhoven.

I've been given the number 35 shirt to reflect my age.
Steve Claridge muses on his shirt number at Millwall.

I prefer players not to be too good or clever at other things. It means they concentrate on football. Former Spurs' boss Bill Nicholson.

We had two players sent off at Newcastle last year for heavy breathing.
Joe Royle

The trouble with football referees is that they know the rules but they don't know the game. Bill Shankly

I've only been booked twice this season. The last one was for doing an impression of the linesmen… I got the other yellow card for winking. Alan Shearer sheds that 'boring' tag.

Leeds United? Most people imagine us as an evil-looking bunch of characters with black capes and handlebar moustaches. Johnny Giles on being part of Revie's Leeds.

Football is not art, but there is an art to playing good football. Rudi Krol *Brilliant Orange*

There is no medal better than being acclaimed for your style. Johann Cruyff *Brilliant Orange:*

I went to the Chelsea training ground and watched Claudio Ranieri, who's a fantastic Italian coach, do exactly the same thing we were doing at Plymouth Argyle. Coaches are coaches. The secret of it all really is man management. Paul Sturrock *The Guardian* 05/03/04

A medal from Princess Di and a kiss from Sam Hammam and with no disrespect to either, you wish it could have been the other way round! Vinnie Jones on receiving his FA Cup winners' medal in 1988.

It is like loading a bullet into the chamber of a gun and asking everyone to pull the trigger. Someone will get the bullet, you know that, and it will reduce them to nothing. Fairness is not even an issue. **Christian Karembeu on penalty shoot-outs.**

All that I know most surely of morality and the obligations of man I owe to football.
Albert Camus

I think capital punishment is a great deterrent.
Tommy Docherty offers a solution to the hooligan problem.

Pele… has done more for goodwill and friendship between nations than all of the ambassadors put together.
J.B. Pinheiro, Brazilian ambassador to the UN.

"What do you think of Brazil?" "I think he's a great player."
Kenny Dalglish 'misunderstands' a journalist at the 1982 World Cup finals.

I have no interest in gardening. If I did I would probably plant my flowers in a 4-4-2 formation. **Tommy Docherty**

When people come to assess my career, I do not want them to judge me on victories or defeats. I want them to say: he played the game, he was fair, he didn't cheat the players or the crowd. If I never cheated them, I never cheated anybody. **Bill Shankly**

David Batty is quite prolific, isn't he? He scores one goal a season, regular as clockwork. **Kenny Dalglish**

I am not condoning the dirty play that Wimbledon have such a name for: but why are their longball tactics considered immoral and a disgrace to the game? If you get beaten in a running race, it is no good complaining that the other person didn't run gracefully enough. **Simon Barnes defends The Crazy Gang.**

He comes with his usual health warning for centre halves. **Keith Gillespie on Blackburn colleague Mark Hughes.**

I have no complaints about Thierry Henry being named double player of the year. He deserved it and I voted for him myself. **Ruud van Nistelrooy at the end of the 2002/03 season.**

D'you think you'll be a player when your voice breaks?

Billy Bremner to Alan Ball during Scotland's 1967 victory against the Auld Enemy.

You'd have a got a better view from the stand.

Bolton's Frank Worthington to Terry Butcher of Ipswich after lifting the ball over his head.
FourFourTwo: 09/02

We, Lakeside United, are a Sunday amateur club and have been formed three years. Despite being of great repute, we need a little more punch and think that Mr Greaves will fit the bill adequately.

Hopeful letter from Lakeside United in Thurrock to Milan, offering to return Jimmy Greaves to the nation, 1961.

If you were a racehorse, they'd shoot you.

Francis Lee implies that the 37-year-old Mike Summerbee is past his best.

How does it feel to be a navvy among artists?

Millwall's Eamonn Dunphy to Villa's Trevor Hockey.

At times I believe Diego [Maradona] is in love with my husband. It must be the long hair and the big muscles. **Marianna Nannis, wife of Argentine star Claudio Caniggia.** *Observer Sport Monthly*

You'd better win this one lads. I need the bonus. I've got a wife, two kids and a budgie to keep. **Alan Gilzean motivates the Tottenham team.**

Even if the next player who provokes me pulls out a gun and shoots me, I'll walk away... or hobble, at least. **Danny Maddix rues a suspension.**

When you have friends in the game you want them to do well… but not as well as you.
Colin Harvey, upon getting the manager's job at Everton, on his predecessor and former team-mate Howard Kendall. Kendall was to succeed Harvey three years later.

I watched the rugby with a former captain of England, Alan Shearer. We were in bed watching it – separate beds. **Gary Speed reveals how he watched England win the rugby World Cup.** *The Guardian* 11/11/03

He's so tiny, I half expected him to come out with a school satchel on his back. If he had, I'd have trodden on his packed lunch.
Wimbledon's Andy Thorn marvels at the diminutive stature of Juninho.

We could have something special here. If he can develop some pace, he's going to be some player. **Terry Owen on his young son Michael.**

Wayne [Rooney] is only seventeen but Sachin Tendulkar didn't become an Indian cricket legend by him being kept back because of his age. **Gary Neville**

The simplest solution is to stop the ball getting to Ronaldo in the first place. If the ball does get to him, we have to make sure he has no space to turn or knock the ball into. And if that doesn't work, we'll have to tie his shoelaces together.
John Collins on Scotland's game plan before the 1998 World Cup opener.

I don't give a damn about records. Kylie Minogue makes records.
Sunderland's Jason McAteer shrugs off the club's losing streak. *The Guardian* 23/08/03

I'd rather buy a Bob the Builder CD for my two-year-old son.
McAteer reviews Roy Keane's autobiography.

Yes, I swear a lot. But the advantage is that having played abroad, I can choose a different language to the referee's.
Jurgen Klinsmann

I just want to ask you fellas; is (sic) there any diving schools in London? Jurgen Klinsmann to the English press on arriving at Spurs.

Next, a man who's fulfilled every schoolboy's dream. He's won the Double, captained England and driven his car into a wall at very high speed. Ladies and gentlemen, Tony Adams! Tony is introduced to the audience on the Kumars at No. 42.

I've been looking for new kitchen curtains for a long time.
Norwegian 'keeper Erik Thorstvedt after swapping jerseys with the colourful Jorge Campo of Mexico. *Observer Sport Monthly*

When you have played at Millwall and seen some of the things that go on there, this should be nothing I can't handle.

Kasey Keller takes the USA v Iran World Cup clash in his stride.

Do you want me to buy a left-back or help save children's lives? I'm not going to do both… go and look in that hospice and have a look at the kids – that's where my money is going.

Robbie Williams reacts to suggestions that he might slip a few bob to home-town Port Vale.
Independent quotes of the year

If the crowd only wants to come and watch models then they should go and buy a copy of Playboy.

Norwegian international Lise Klaveness with a sideswipe at Sepp Blatter.
The Guardian 16/01/04

It's a top club but it's not a top, top, top club.

Jimmy Floyd Hasselbaink on Chelsea's position in footballing society.

I scored for Liverpool on the opening day of the season… a 'big balls' goal.

Paolo di Canio on big…er…balls.

A real player can always make a monkey out of a gorilla.

Rangers legend Jim Baxter.

Jesus, I only wanted you to pass the salt.

Roy Keane reacts to a tactical talk from Tony Adams at a UEFA dinner. *Independent* quotes of the year

We used to joke in the United dressing room that he was the only player in the League who had to have turn-ups on his shorts. **George Best on the diminutive Bobby Collins of Leeds.**

Someone asked me last week if I missed the Villa. I said 'No, I live in one.' **David Platt on swapping Birmingham for Bari.**

In Glasgow half the football fans hate you and the other half think they own you.

Tommy Burns

Watch a Brazilian pass the ball. No lofted centre from the wing for him, no forty-yard long-balls that need only to be a yard out to be wasted. Tom Finney

If there were 22 Matthews on the pitch, I'd be out of a job.

Referee Arthur Ellis on the unblemished disciplinary record of Stanley Matthews.

Playing Stan is like playing a ghost.

Manchester United's Johnny Carey on Stanley Matthews.

Leeds went a goal ahead and, sure enough, the ball boys disappeared.

Ex-referee Keith Hackett notes gamesmanship at Elland Road.

A top referee is an official who treats a player like a man.

Ron Harris

I do it because I was a useless player.

Jim Rushton on his motivation to make it as a League referee.

Even when they had Moore, Hurst and Peters, West Ham's average finish was about seventeenth. It just shows how crap the other eight of us were.

Harry Redknapp

He was involved in both and spent so much time on the ground I was wondering when his funeral would be held. **FIFA assessor Keith Cooper on Ashley Cole's role in red cards for Leeds' Danny Mills and Lee Bowyer.**

Five days thou shalt labour, as the Bible says. The seventh day is the Lord thy God's. The sixth day is for football. **Anthony Burgess**

Football is all very well as a game for rough girls, but is hardly suitable for delicate boys. **Oscar Wilde**

Football is the opera of the people. Stafford Heginbotham, former Bradford City chairman.

The rules are very simple, basically it is this: if it moves, kick it. If it doesn't move, kick it until it does. **Soccer writer Phil Woosnam puts it in a nutshell.**

In a world haunted by the hydrogen and napalm bomb, the football field is a place where sanity and hope are still unmolested. Stanley Rous, 1952.

What a player! Even when he farts he scores a goal.
Alessandro del Piero savours Ruud van Nistelrooy.

People say his first touch isn't good, but he usually scores with his second.

Wolves manager Graham Turner offers an assessment of Steve Bull.

As we went out on the pitch he handed me a piece of paper. It was the evening menu for the Liverpool Royal Infirmary.

Jimmy Greaves recalls an Anfield encounter with Tommy Smith.

Rumour has it that when Julian Dicks moved to Liverpool he picked up the number 23 shirt because it said Fowler on it. Football writer Kevin Baldwin.

It's bloody hard work being true to the real values.
Bill Shankly

There's no such thing as staleness. It's just a name given to the state of mind of some players. It doesn't exist if their will is fresh.
Tommy Docherty

All a manager has to do is to keep eleven players happy. The eleven in the reserves. The first team are happy because they're the first team. Rodney Marsh

It's bad players who are the luxury, not the skillful ones.
Danny Blanchflower, on hearing whispers that he might be a liability.

Bob Wilson [needs] to go on a crash course in basic communication techniques so he'll grasp that if you ask someone a question you have to give them longer than five seconds to answer before interrupting. One of the list of demands printed by fanzine *When Saturday Comes* in its 1996 tenth birthday issue.

I believe that international football between representative teams is on the way out. Its days are numbered and it will disappear completely just as soon as we get a full programme of international football at club level. Jimmy Greaves in 1962.

Look laddie, if you're in the penalty area and aren't quite sure what to do with the ball, just stick it in the net and we'll discuss your options afterwards. Bill Shankly

Playing against English clubs is like when your mother forced you to eat vegetables when you didn't like it. You have to suffer a bit if you want to be strong. Hernan Crespo in his pre-Chelsea days.

Our goalscoring is like ketchup, you never know how much is going to come out of the bottle.

Club Brugge manager Trond Sollied.

I think that clocking into a factory would be the worst thing in the world. All you could say to the man next to you is 'What's in your sandwich, Charlie?'.

Rodney Marsh muses on his escape, 1967.

Chris Cattlin is a very complex mixture of a man who could alternate between Mussolini and Bambi depending on which day you caught him. Frank Worthington's verdict on his ex-Brighton manager.

I'm a people's man, a player's man. You could call me a humanist.
Bill Shankly

In our interview with Sir Jack Hayward, the chairman of Wolverhampton Wanderers, page 20, Sport, yesterday, we mistakenly attributed to him the following comment: 'Our team was the worst in the First Division and I'm sure it will be the worst in the Premiership'. *The Guardian* 12/08/03

Maybe I will phone Cudicini at Chelsea and also Gattuso, Amoruso and all the other 'usos'. Scotland manager Berti Vogts, reacting to suggestions that changes in the residency law could qualify some better players for Scotland. *Independent* 21/02/04

I'd like to get ten goals a season but the authorities don't normally let me play for a whole season.

Vinnie Jones

Addicted by Tony Adams, CollinsWillow, 1998.

A Funny Thing Happened on my Way to Spurs by Jimmy Greaves, Nicholas Kaye Ltd., 1962.

An Autobiography by Pat Jennings in association with Reg Drury, Willow Books, 1983.

Baxter: The Party s Over Jim Baxter in Association with John Fargrieve, Stanley Paul, 1984.

Becks Talking Omnibus Press, 2002

Blue Blood: The Mike Doyle Story Mike Doyle and David Clayton, The Parrs Wood Press, 2004.

Brilliant Orange: The Neurotic Genius of Dutch Football by David Winner, Bloomsbury, 2000

Cloughie: The Autobiography Partridge Press, 1994.

Cloughie: Walking on Water Headline, 2002

David Beckham: My Side — The Autobiography David Beckham, HarperCollinsWillow. 2003.

Do That Again Son And I ll Break Your Legs Phil Thompson, Virgin Books, 1996

Fathers, Sons and Football by Colin Shindler, Headline, 2001.

Football Confidential 2 by David Conn, Chris Green, Richard McIlroy and Kevin Mousley, BBC Worldwide Ltd, 2003

Footballers Haircuts: The Illustrated History Cris Freddi, Weidenfeld Nicolson. 2003.

Forward with Leeds by Jonny Giles, Stanley Paul, 1970.

Futebol the Brazilian Way of Life by Alex Bellos, Bloomsbury, 2002.

Geoff Hurst: 1966 and All That Headline, 2001

George Best, The Good, The Bad and the Bubbly by George Best and Ross Benson, Pan Books, 1991.

Hackett s Law: A Referee s Notebook by Keith Hackett, Willow Books, 1986.

Ian Rush: My Italian Diary by Ian Rush, Arthur Barker, 1989.

Power, Corruption and Pies: A Decade of the Best Football Writing from WSC Two Heads Publishing, 1997.

Martin O Neill The Biography by Alex Montgomery, Virgin Books, 2003.

Manchester United Ruined my Life by Colin Shindler, Headline, 1998.

Match Annual, 2004 Hayden Publishing, 2003.

Michael Owen s Soccer Skills by Michael Owen with Dave Harrison, CollinsWillow, 1999.

Mr Wright by Ian Wright, CollinsWillow, 1996.